glimpse

glimpse

Publication of
The Society for Phenomenology and Media
Vol. 20, 2019

The Society for Phenomenology and Media
Glimpse is the annual publication of the Society for Phenomenology and Media.

The author retains copyright of any paper published in this issue of *Glimpse*. Permission for republication can be obtained from the Editor at glimpseSPM@gmail.com.

Republication must include a note citing the relevant issue of *Glimpse* as the place of original publication.

Copyright © 2019

All rights reserved.
ISBN-13: 978-1-7340540-0-2

SPM Officers (2018 – 2019)
President: Lars Lundsten
Vice President: Cristina Pontes Bonfiglioli
Secretary: Elvira Godek-Kiryluk
Treasurer: Luis Acebal

SPM Board of Directors (2018 – 2019)
Luis Acebal, National University, Redding, California, USA
Cristina Pontes Bonfiglioli, Centro Interdisciplinar de Semiótica da Cultura e da Mídia, Pontifical Catholic University of São Paulo, São Paulo, Brazil
Melinda Campbell, National University, La Jolla, California, USA
Alberto José Luis Carrillo Canán (Chair), Benemérita Universidad Autónoma de Puebla, Mexico
Gerardo de la Fuente, Universidad Nacional Autónoma de Mexico, Mexico City, Mexico
Alejandra de las Mercedes Fernández, Universidad Nacional del Nordeste, Resistencia, Argentina
Elvira Godek-Kiryluk, University of Illinois at Chicago, Chicago, USA
Jacques Ibanez Bueno, Université Savoie Mont Blanc, Chambéry, France
Stacey O'Neal Irwin, Millersville University of Pennsylvania, Millersville, Pennsylvania, USA
Matti Itkonen, University of Jyväskylä, Jyväskylä, Finland
Pieter Lemmens, Radboud University Nijmegen, Nijmegen, Netherlands
Nicola Liberati (Vice Chair), University of Twente, Enschede, Netherlands
Lars Lundsten, University of Akureyri, Akureyri, Iceland
Paul Majkut, National University, La Jolla, California, USA
Nyasha Mboti, University of Johannesburg, Johannesburg, South Africa
Shoji Nagataki, Chukyo University, Nagoya, Japan
José David Romero Martin, University of the Basque Country, Bilbao, Spain
Randall Dana Ulveland, Western Oregon University, Monmouth, Oregon, USA
Yoni Van Den Eede, Free University of Brussels, Brussels, Belgium
Tõnu Viik, Tallinn University, Tallinn, Estonia

SPM Advisory (2018 – 2019)
Mónica E. Alarcón Dávila, Universidad de Antioquia, Medellín, Columbia
Bas de Boer, University of Twente, Enschede, Netherlands
Adriana Durán Guerrero, Benemérita Universidad Autónoma de Puebla, Escuela de Artes Plásticas y Audiovisuales, Puebla, Mexico
Luanne Frank, University of Texas at Arlington, Arlington, Texas, USA
Miguel A. García, Hochschule Furtwangen, Furtwangen im Schwarzwald, Germany
Sophia Siddique Harvey, Vassar College, Poughkeepsie, New York, USA
Hye Young Kim, Husserl Archive, Ecole Normale Supérieure, Paris, France
Olga Kudina, University of Twente, Enschede, Netherlands
Sarah Lwahas, University of Jos, Plateau State, Jos, Nigeria
Lisa Neville, State University of New York, Cortland, USA
Obiageli Pauline Ohiagu, University of Port Harcourt, Nigeria
Melentie Pandilovski, Riddoch Art Gallery, Mount Gambier, Australia
Tracy Powell, Western Oregon University, Monmouth, Oregon, USA
Marleni Reyes Monreal, Benemérita Universidad Autónoma de Puebla, Escuela de Artes Plásticas y Audiovisuales, Puebla, Mexico
Dennis Skocz, Independent Scholar, Washington D. C., USA
James Steinhoff, University of Western Ontario, London, Ontario, Canada
T.J. Thomson, FHEA, Queensland University of Technology, Brisbane, Australia
Tales Tomaz, University of Salzburg, Salzburg, Austria
Marta Graciela Trógolo, Universidad Nacional del Nordeste, Resistencia, Chaco, Argentina
May Zindel, Unarte University, Puebla, Mexico

***Glimpse* Editors:** Elvira Godek-Kiryluk, *Managing Editor*
Melinda Campbell, *Assistant Editor*

GLIMPSE

Contents

Introduction   9
    Paul Majkut

Keynote Address: Circuits of Apartheid: A Plea for Apartheid Studies   15
    Nyasha Mboti

We are our mobile screen … "We wear all mankind as our skin": The Mobile Phone and the Structure of Experience   71
    Alberto José Luis Carrillo Canán

My Data Is Mine: What Is the Meaning of Participation in Data Capitalism?   79
    João Carlos Correia

Global Media Literacy: A Conceptual Error and Eight Typologies   89
    Ulaş Başar Gezgin

EXPLORING THE DIGITAL ATTITUDE: WHERE FORM AND CONTENT BLUR STACEY O'NEAL IRWIN	99
ALEXA DOES NOT CARE. SHOULD YOU? MEDIA LITERACY IN THE AGE OF DIGITAL VOICE ASSISTANTS OLGA KUDINA	107
NOTES ON MEDIA LITERACY AND ILLITERACY PAUL MAJKUT	117
DIGITAL DISSENT ON WIKILEAKS: ANONYMOUS WHISTLEBLOWERS IN THE SHADOW OF JULIAN ASSANGE RIANKA ROY	125
THE MOLD IS THE MESSAGE: MEDIA LITERACY VS. MEDIA HEALTH YONI VAN DEN EEDE	135
CONTRIBUTORS	143

Introduction

The Twentieth International Conference of the Society for Phenomenology and Media took place at the University of Akureyri (*Háskólinn á Akureyri*) in Akureyri, Iceland.

Akureyri, a small city in the north of the country located on a beautiful Fjord, is graced by spectacular landscape and stunning *Aurora borealis,* and it is these Northern Lights that may serve as the motif of the conference: night light that illuminates the dark with unusual brilliance.

Though the climate was exceptionally cold to those who attended the conference, the university greeted participants with warmth and hospitality. Our host, Professor Lars Lundsten, brought together a diverse group of speakers from around the world as well as affording the opportunity for the free expression of widespread philosophical approaches. The theme of the conference, "'Global Media Literacy in the Digital Age," drew a variety of approaches to the topic, often sharply contrasting, always collegial. If a division of thought was apparent, it may be summarized as a difference between traditional epistemological and contemporary socio-economic approaches. This dialectic provided the conference with lively exchanges during ample panel follow-up discussion.

The essays included in this edition of *Glimpse* have been selected by a process of double-blind review. A first screening of all papers submitted for publication reduces the number to fifteen. This process includes three reviewers. A second screening takes place, narrowing the selection further. In addition, papers received by an open call for papers for publication—aimed at those not attending the SPM conference and not SPM members—are reviewed. In this edition of *Glimpse,* three such papers are included. While every participant in the conference is entitled to submit for publication in *Glimpse,* they all undergo the same selection process. Those not selected for inclusion in *Glimpse* are published in a separate SPM journal, *Proceedings of the Twentieth Annual International Conference of the Society for Phenomenology and Media.* The essays in both publications are arranged in alphabetical order.

In a sense, the tone of the conference was set by the keynote speaker, Professor Nyasha Mboti, of the Department of Communication Studies at the University of Johannesburg, South Africa. His current research, framing the emergence of a new theoretical paradigm for Apartheid Studies, set the intellectual parameters for all that followed.

As you read Prof. Mboti's keynote, "Circuits of Apartheid: A Plea for Apartheid Studies," you will note his highly systematic style of thought that, again and again, "returns to the things themselves" in a manner not unfamiliar to phenomenologists. His use of historical data serves as a ground for his overall theory. Close observation of details brings his thought back to that ground. Often, he disabuses his audience of preconceived and uncritical assumptions. For example, in countering the reactionary attitude towards the poor that suggests that they need to understand the importance of a planned budget, he removes the ideological blindfold that often keeps philosophers from seeing "things in themselves," replying that the have-nots of the world do not need lectures from the haves on family budgeting. The poor are expert at budgeting, a necessity for daily survival. Indeed, it is the rich who need lessons on justice and a "balanced budget."

In the following pages, the division between socio-econo-political thought and epistemological attitudes towards global media literacy can be seen in two groups of essays. It should be pointed out, however, that the tradition in SPM is that participants are free to write on *any* aspect of media. SPM conference participants are free to ignore conference themes—as long as their papers are concerned with media in a broad sense.

If, for convenience, we may divide the papers in this volume into two groups, we find the following in what we may call the "epistemological group":

- José Luis Carrillo Canán: "We Are Our Mobile Screen … 'We Wear All Mankind as Our Skin': The Mobile Phone and the Structure of Experience."
- Ulaş Başar Gezgin: "Global Media Literacy: A Conceptual Error and Eight Typologies."
- Stacey O'Neal Irwin: "Exploring the Digital Attitude: Where Form and Content Blur."
- Yoni Van Den Eede: "The Mold Is the Message: Media Literacy vs. Media Health."

The other grouping, the socio-econo-political, contains the remaining essays:

- Nyasha Mboti: "Circuits of Apartheid: A Plea for Apartheid Studies."
- João Carlos Correia: "Data Is Mine: What Is the Meaning of Participation in Data Capitalism?"
- Olga Kudina: "Alexa Does Not Care. Should You? Media Literacy in the Age of Digital Voice Assistants."
- Paul Majkut: "Media Literacy and Illiteracy."
- Rianka Roy: "Digital Dissent on WikiLeaks: Anonymous Whistleblowers in the Shadow of Julian Assange."

Professors Canán and van den Eede both take up epistemological questions of just how the user is subsumed by digital media, how digital technology shapes experience, and the relationship of iPhone and Internet devices and their users. Both essays show the influence of Marshall McLuhan. We are reminded that McLuhan, speaking of television, held that *the viewer is the screen,* and that the medium itself is the message that shape the user.

While Ulaş Başar Gezgin's essay is placed here in the epistemological group, the thrust of his argument is to critique the theme of the conference, global media literacy. Diving deeply into the topic, he finds eight forms of conceptual error underlying the framing of the theme. In this, he shares a similar position to Majkut, who is easily identified in the socio-econo-political group.

Stacey Irwin returns us to solid epistemological media concerns. In the fashion of Husserl's phenomenological understanding of the natural attitude, Irwin considers the age-old problem of the inseparable relationship of content and form. She speaks of a "blur" line between the two. Since the separation of content and form is done purely for purposes of theoretical analysis and an impossibility in practice, her argument reminds us that the two categories are solely attitudes towards something, not a division that exists in the thing itself.

Each of the essays in the socio-econo-political group contains, either by suggestion or overtly, advocacy of a position towards digital media. And each inherently asks questions of value, not only epistemological mechanics. The underlying sentiment of these essays is ethical and political, assuming that politics is ethics writ large. The essays in this group implicitly and explicitly argue that social action cannot be separated from theorizing—that praxis precedes theory, that all knowledge arises from the senses.

The call for Apartheid Studies made by Prof. Nyasha Mboti takes two forms. First, it uncovers and dismisses long-held misconceptions concerning questions of racial injustices and the residue of colonial oppression. Second, it proposes a concrete plan for developing an academic discipline. It was greeted enthusiastically by Majkut, who saw parallels to his own call for studies of the internal colony.

João Carlos Correia cuts to the root of the problem of digital media by placing it in the context of history and contemporary capitalism in "Data Is Mine: What Is the Meaning of Participation in Data Capitalism?" Here, we learn that the digital consumer is the first consumed.

The potential dangers of digital communications are considered in Olga Kudina's "Alexa Does Not Care. Should You? Media Literacy in the Age of Digital Voice Assistants." The ethical undertones inherent in technology are faced, the question of just what "literacy" means is posed, and the distinction between the AI transhuman and the human delved by implication.

Paul Majkut believes that media "literacy" alone cannot explain digital practice because its unspoken opposite, illiteracy, is ignored, making for prejudice against those who cannot "read" and "write" in digital media.

Rianka Roy brings discussion of media literacy back to earth in his discussion of WikiLeaks and the significance of anonymous whistleblowers made possible by Julian Assange.

The counter-positioning of fundamental differences on how media should be approached not only made for a lively conference but widened the intellectual grasp of the Society.

SPM has always been a unique combination of philosophers and media theorists. What philosophers could not explain in terms of concrete practice, media theorists made clear. When media theorists neglected placing their theories in a larger context, philosophers took up the challenge.

The conference at the University of Akureyri was a test of the resiliency of SPM. The Twentieth International Conference of the Society for Phenomenology and Media in 2018 was planned for Winnipeg, Canada, but unforeseen problems meant a last-minute change. Prof. Lars Lundsten, an original founding member of SPM, stepped into the void and volunteered to host the conference. The policy of SPM is that our conferences rotate: Europe, North America, and Latin America. 2018 was set for the North American conference and, since Iceland is neither a part of Europe nor North America, it was a happy coincidence for which the Society is deeply indebted to Professor Lundsten and the University of Akureyri.

—Paul Majkut

GLIMPSE

GLIMPSE

Keynote Address

Circuits of Apartheid:
A Plea for Apartheid Studies

NYASHA MBOTI

UNIVERSITY OF JOHANNESBURG
JOHANNESBURG, SOUTH AFRICA

ABSTRACT: *This keynote address is about the supply, maintenance and allocation of fungible, vulnerable human bodies—what American President Donald Trump would categorize as the shitholes of the world. Underlying our modern times is a large, unsolved problem about what is really going on in the world. I use the novel theoretical lens of Apartheid Studies to appreciate how we have neglected to read, recognize and call out the persistent circuits of apartheid that are at the heart of global capitalist modernity. Our contemporary age, built on interoperable digital networks, tends to reinforce global forms of apartheid. Apartheid Studies is a new field of studies that makes it possible to expose these circuits. Whereas human beings are human because we all possess a kind of strongly encrypted* password *which we reserve to give or not to give—so that we feel relatively protected and free to be what we want—this password protection has been eroded by institutions and powerful elites. Modernity itself, by its very nature, emerges when we start to share our passwords with strangers. Passing on the control of the* passwords *of our being to strangers causes global apartheid. Global capitalist modernity, expressed in invasive technology, generally undermines human beings' sense of self, immunity, inviolability, indivisibility, and replaces it with social media and an internet of things which are predicated on sharing our privacy with strangers. I propose new emphases on restorative forensics and literacies that are appropriate to the task of generating a scholarship of the future that is ethical and opposed to systemic injustice, that exposes global exploitation, racism, deception, and corruption, and that promotes just worlds.*

KEYWORDS: Apartheid; Apartheid Studies; blackbodies; state of password exemption; dead zones; state of exemption; circuits of the occult.

INTRODUCTION

This Keynote Address is on a subject that is, remarkably, uncharted territory. Strange but true: there is no field of studies called Apartheid Studies *anywhere* in the whole wide world.[1] The absence does not make any sense at all. There is no degree

---

[1] Despite the epistemic neglect of the concept of apartheid, various scholars have identified manifestations of apartheid since the antiquity (Lewis 1983; Löwstedt 2014; Bathish & Löwstedt 1999), and in places as varied as Ptolemaic Egypt (Löwstedt 2014; Bathish & Löwstedt 1999), 20th century South Africa, present day Israel (Clarno

program or even an apology of an undergraduate course or module called "Apartheid Studies." There is not a single Center for Apartheid Studies, Institute of Apartheid Studies, or Research Chair in Apartheid Studies. Not a single theoretical framework has emerged out of the paradigm of apartheid. Why is there so little interest in formally provisioning for the systematic study of apartheid? Try as I might, I can find no worse case of paradigm neglect in the world of scholarship. The real reason for the neglect will perhaps become clearer by the end of the address, but by then I hope to have made a sensible case for establishing Apartheid Studies. The lack of a strong and robust scholarship that *specifically* and *systematically* studies and theorizes *apartheid* troubles me, as does the sense that apartheid persists beyond its assumed death in South Africa in the early 1990s.

The first sign of trouble was the shooting of 34 miners by police at Lonmin in August 2012. Something told me that the bloodshed of the miners, the miners' demand for a wage of R12.500, the role of the corporation of London Minerals (Lonmin), and the police who opened fire on the miners *were all linked* by a golden thread. What was this *golden thread*? Since 16 August 2012, I had been searching for the golden thread. Like the Schrödinger's cat, this thread seemed *both* there and not there. Why were 30 million South Africans—half the population—living in dire poverty in possibly the richest country on the continent? Why was there poverty, on such a scale, side by side with so much affluence? Why had the police in 2012, after being instructed in an email by the then Deputy President of the country to take "concomitant action," shot at striking miners killing at least 34 of them? What is "concomitant action"? Why are dozens of children dying in shack fires across the country every year? Why did a five-year-old boy, Michael Komape, drown in feces in a pit latrine at his school? What sort of ineffable *algorithm* underlies all these facts?

There has been no recognition of apartheid as a field of study or as a theoretical paradigm, and no attempt to assess what apartheid *really is* and *what it really means*. There has also been no concomitant interest in studying how apartheid metamorphoses, adapts, and moves with the times. I proceed, in this keynote address, from the claim that it is certainly possible, on the basis of a renewed definition of apartheid, to identify apartheid as an *algorithmic* global paradigm (i.e. step by step and precise *telling apart* and *keeping*

2017; Pappé 2004, 2006, 2014; Löwstedt 2014; Bathish & Löwstedt 1999; UN 2017), and Anglo-Saxon England (Pattison 2008). Others have identified apartheid in places as far flung as Hawaii (Conklin 2007), Canada (Galabuzi 2006), Brazil (Lowy 2003; Verrisimo 1994; Brandão 1998), France (Collon 2005; Vidal 2005), United States (Massey & Denton 1993), Palestine (Clarno 2017; Pappé 2004, 2006, 2014) and India (Teltumbde 2010; CHR & GJ 2007), and in fields such as medicine (Washington 2006), urbanisation (Massey & Denton 1993; Vidal 2005), epistemology (Rabaka 2010), neoliberalism (Clarno 2017), and so on. There is also a vibrant cross-continental debate since the 1973 Apartheid Convention and the 1998 Rome Statute about whether apartheid has gained customary status as an international crime against humanity (Lingaas 2015, 2017; Eden, 2014; Booysen 1976; Kittichaisaree 2001; Cassese 2008; Bultz 2013).

apart of human beings for purposes of keeping the dominant social, political, and economic order from reaching the threshold of true crisis), which more or less marches in step with parasitic modernity, and which sheds light on the deep algorithms which underlie global capitalist modernity from Australia to the United States, Canada to Brazil, Bulgaria to Kenya, China to India, Israel to Zimbabwe, and so on. Boesak (2015) has rightly identified apartheid in its global guises and linked it with the idea of *kairos* and *crisis*. Apartheid Studies as a field develops a *threshold model* that presumes the existence of i) apartheid crime scenes, ii) apartheid algorithms, and iii) a definitive cut-off point of crisis which apartheid never quite reaches because it metamorphoses and hides in plain sight.

The choice to use the term apartheid is solely mine, because I see it as singularly the most evocative in describing the phenomena by which global capitalist modernity secures itself. Although by no means the only or the most important motivation, my location in South Africa has played some part in the adoption of this word. Certainly, the notion of apartheid is incredibly useful beyond its narrow technical application. Apartheid—Dutch or Afrikaans for "apartness"—is a technical term for a highly developed system of regulating, organizing, *allocating* and *maintaining* blackbodies that existed in 20th century South Africa. Basically, whites in South Africa were faced with the insoluble dilemma that all colonizers around the globe face: how to make those whom they colonize *be-without-being*, or at least *be there without being visible*. That is, the whites' dilemma was how best to make the colonized *foot* the bill and *meet* the cost of their own colonization. White people in South Africa wanted black people to be *perpetually available* to be exploited, but they did not want that *perpetual availability*—a kind of occult *intransitive being*—to come at a cost to the whites. Rather, the costs of apartheid had to be borne by the oppressed *themselves*. Hence, they created a perpetual motion machine of the first kind: *apartheid*. Apartheid was the formal system created to turn blacks into *intransitive beings* and thus resolve the paradox of making them *be there but not be there*. This algorithm would take human lives and transform them into a *cost-absorbing intransitivity*.

The algorithm of apartheid would seek to achieve the *cost-absorbing intransitivity* of black people through one of the most detailed, most total, and most degrading systems for controlling human beings ever developed. This included the creation of a phalanx of laws regulating "separate development," the perpetual removal of people, the creation of townships, hostels and homelands, job reservations, and so on, in order to make blacks *be there but not be there*. That is, apartheid was intended to definitively *cut out the cost* that comes with blacks *being-there* as full human beings. Whites wanted blacks to *always be there*—to always be available—to be exploited, while at the same time refusing to accept the natural cost that any *always being-there* of humans brings. In other words, apartheid tried to formalize the violation of the principle that everything comes with a cost. It is apartheid that gives us a definitive name for the practice of definitively cutting out costs: making those who carry the burden pay the cost of carrying the burden. At the heart of apartheid, therefore, is this broader, sinister illogic: to *invoice* the costs of oppression to the oppressed themselves, *bill* slaves for slavery, and *levy* the poor for being poor.

All said, the term apartheid is today badly delexicalized, neglected, and underused. What I am attempting to do here is to *relexicalize* it. Other people may prefer different terms and emphases. This is okay. To my mind, the more important issue (certainly more important than quibbling about terminology) is to finally be able to systematically study certain overdue, but fundamental questions about the true nature of our modern times.

II

Human beings are not substances. They cannot, for instance, be put in a test tube in order to make them *behave* in a certain way or to see how they *react* in given situations. Those who desire to make human beings behave in certain ways or observe how they react in certain situations have thus had to innovate: they have had to turn human beings *themselves* into test tubes. We are familiar with how scientists experiment with animals in labs: when they desire to make a living thing such as a guinea pig or a plant behave *in a certain way*, they place a foreign substance in its body, or they simply manipulate its surroundings. Unlike in a laboratory where a scientist gets a reaction from bringing substances into contact with each other, in the worlds of human beings just about everything is achieved by manipulating our humanity.

The claim that every person on earth is indivisibly human ultimately means something special: that we all possess a kind of strongly encrypted password which we reserve to give or not to give. When we are this human, we feel relatively protected and free to be what we want. However, this password protection has been persistently eroded by institutions and powerful elites. Modernity, by its very nature, emerges when we start to share our passwords with strangers. The concepts of network society, stock exchange, free market, capitalism, globalization, social media, or the internet of things, for instance, are possible only when the passwords of our being have been passed on and are known, managed, allocated, and even owned by strangers.

A beggar rummages in a dustbin. A homeless person curls to sleep under a bridge. A boat full of "illegal" immigrants capsizes in the Mediterranean. A civilian is beaten up by the police. Food for refugees is dropped from an airplane. These are familiar scenes that define the data of *telling apart*. People, legally or illegally, cross fences, borders and other *trespass zones* because such zones generate data that enable institutions to *tell* human beings *apart* from one another. To *cross* a trespass zone is therefore to render such data inoperative. That is, merely by crossing borders we concretely set aside *separation* from other human beings, *separation* from the fun that we want to have, and *separation* from livelihoods. The point here is that human lives, actions and ethics are bound up with *separations*. By default, all action, reaction, cause, effect, behavior change, social change, and identity, are all functions of *separation*. That is, we are what we are *either* because we are where we want to be and have what we want *or* because we are not where we want to be and do not have what we want. Whoever we are, wherever we may be, we all react to *separation*, and are unavoidably conditioned by it. Our everyday worlds, the traditions we cherish, and the things we do, from the tiniest to the largest, are bound up with all this universe of *telling apart*.

Telling apart is critical to understanding what is going on in the world precisely because it deploys a very singular, transformative feature: a *state of password exemption*. It is this state of exemption that, for instance, gives a homeless person *unlimited access* to the underside of a bridge. Without *password exemption*, the underside of a bridge will remain the underside of a bridge, and not *transform* into a "house" or home. The underside of a bridge cannot become a home *until* and *unless* the password protected *meaning* of home is messed with, tampered with, and *let go*. This act of *letting go* explains the state of password exemption. Only by *letting go the passwords of our being* can a structure that is not a home (such as the underside of a bridge, a hole in the ground, a piece of tarpaulin, or a plastic-and-cardboard shack) become a home. That is, only by subjecting the definition of home to drastic, transformative *exemption* and *re-evaluation* can the underside of a bridge or a piece of tarpaulin ever become a home. Beggars rummage in the dust bins for a meal precisely by giving up their claims (their passwords) to a proper, hot meal. A rickety, leaky, overcrowded boat becomes the site of transport and passage to an assumed better life in Europe *if* and *only if* one enters a *state of password exemption*. Without such transformative password exemption – that is, without arbitrarily adjusting human value—it is not possible for a human being to eat from a dustbin, to live in a shack, or to accept a minimum wage.

This globalized *password exemption*, which works by precisely and arbitrarily manipulating the constitutive *meaningfulness* of things, is what we call *apartheid*. Apartheid simply refers to the data by which we tell human beings apart from other human beings, such that it becomes *inevitable* that some human beings will capsize in a boat, eat from dustbins, sleep under a bridge, live on a minimum wage, work in a sweatshop, and live in a township, barrio, slum, or favela, and so on. Indeed, it is inevitable that someone is sleeping under a bridge or in a plastic-and-cardboard "house" as you read this sentence. It is inevitable that a child has just died from malnutrition this very second. It is not merely possible but inevitable that millions of people are working in sweatshops this very moment. It is inevitable that hundreds of thousands have just been retrenched from their jobs as we speak; millions have succumbed to preventable diseases; millions have gone to bed hungry, and so on. At the same time, it is inevitable that billions of dollars, yuan, pounds, rands, and renminbi in wealth have exchanged hands on the stock exchange this very second. Trillions of dollars, yuan, pounds, rands, and renminbi in the form of capital are in circulation as we speak and are being invested and reinvested. The sky has not fallen. The earth still circles the sun. Life goes on. That is, we live in a world where the sky will not fall *just because* of the suffering, trauma and pain borne by the bodies of others, the injustice visited on them, the disposability of their lives, and the uselessness of their existence. By *inevitability* I simply mean that, ultimately, we live in times where injustice and the suffering of *large numbers* of people has already been factored into the equations, calculations, models, blueprints, and *algorithms* of modernity. That is, there is no reason to do away with injustice or the slavery, trauma, and pain of others. Proof of this is that the sky has not fallen. It is not that we *cannot do without* injustice or the slavery, trauma, and pain of others. Apparently not. It is not that, in the grand scheme of things, the *sacrifice* of others is now too valuable to let go. Such an explanation would amount to nothing more than a conspiracy theory—gigabytes of which are dumped every hour on YouTube. Rather, there seems to be the simplest of explanations why things are the way they are in the modern world: it is that *the sky has not fallen*. This also happens to be the simplest definition of apartheid. Life goes on, still. There is no conspiracy theory. There is no need of one.

We thus live in a world where it is not merely *possible*, nor just *expected*, but it is *inevitable* that large numbers of human beings will live their lives in dead zones and death zones. This *inevitability* constitutes the prime engine and algorithm of our modern times. And, because of it, you will thus find *apartheid* in any country in the world, at any point in history, in any situation or circumstance, big or small, visible or invisible. After all, modernity itself is only possible on the basis of *apartheid*.

Because it is built from alienating the self, modernity accepts as true the principle that certain of us will *inevitably* suffer losses in our humanity. The problem is that there is no agreement about how much password loss is okay. The world can thus be divided into two categories. The first category consists of those who believe that people who suffer losses have an infinite capacity for suffering. We will call these the *infinites*. The second group are those who believe that people deprived of their passwords have a finite capacity for suffering. We will call them the *finites*. The *finites* want safeguards and argue that the future of the world is dependent on how well we conserve and maintain, in tolerable shape, those who suffer loss. The *finites* are always warning us about pushing the poor (or the climate, etc.) too far. Into this group go the United Nations, human rights organizations, liberals, democratic governments, all manner of sustainability initiatives, and so on. The *infinites*, for their part, believe that safeguards are a sentimental waste of time since suffering people can tolerate literally any loss. This group wants power and profit at all costs. Into this group go most capitalists and dictatorial regimes.

In practice, the relationship between *finites* and *infinites* is an oversimplification, because the two categories overlap a great deal, and there is no clear-cut separation in the end. For instance, some people may think in *finite*-like ways but behave *infinitely*-like and vice versa. Others may not like the suffering they see around them but reason that there is no other way. Some *infinites* may see how deformed people are by loss of their passwords but reason that there are too many people in the world to begin with, and those who are deformed by suffering can be replaced by new births. Other *finites* may accept that certain infinite ideas *do* have merit and can work in a finite-like way with checks and balances and moderation. And so on. There is no contradiction in all this. What is clear is that one can define most existing schools of thought, published opinion, ideas, industries, political theory, philosophy, academic fields and disciplines, and what not, into these two broad divisions: *finite* and *infinite*.

What is lacking in this equation of the *finites* and the *infinites* is the truth of those who suffer losses of their passwords. Whether these people suffer infinitely or finitely is beside the point: for them, loss of self—in whatever amount, form or degree—is not okay. The fact that people may be resilient in the face of loss of their passwords does not constitute a justification. Lost human lives are not an opportunity to debate or theorize whether suffering is infinitely tolerable or how much suffering is tolerable. The truth is that those who carry the cost want the suffering that is going on in this world to stop today. The people who have lost their passwords are the people I shall term *blackbodies*.

In physics, a blackbody is a perfectly absorbent body. Both *finites* and *infinites* arbitrarily regard those who suffer losses of immunity as perfectly *absorbent* and do not so much mind if *blackbodies* absorb blows and crises of modernity. This is because neither *finites* nor *infinites* must live the kinds of password-deprived, password-exempt lives that blackbodies live, eat the food that they eat, work where they work, sleep where they sleep, or die the kinds of deaths they die. It is much easier in life to be a *finite* or an *infinite*, rather than be a password-less *blackbody*. No one wants to be a *blackbody*, although *finites* and *infinites* make it their business to allocate passwords and tell blackbodies how to live and where to live.

The evidence is all round us. There is lots and lots of money being made on the Johannesburg Stock Exchange in South Africa, but how many have ever seen those billions? How many South Africans are suffering from depression, mental illness and stress due to financial problems and not being able to make ends meet? How many have contemplated suicide? There are no statistics, but in the province of Mpumalanga in 2015, a 42-year old woman, her two children and a 17-year old niece made a pact: they chose to kill themselves rather than continue to live the rest of their lives in a House of Hunger, as author Dambudzo Marechera would have called it: a place where the black skin is replaced by stitches on top of more stitches. The family of 4 was exhausted, tired of the blows of never affording anything they needed to live as human beings. The mother and niece succeeded in taking their own lives. The other two children survived and were hospitalized. The acting Premier of the province expressed shock at the "poverty suicides," stating that the act of terminating one's own life because of poverty "is not acceptable" and, indeed, "is a criminal offence because we all have a right to life" (Khosa).[2] The police spokesman in the province "warn[ed] community members to inform authorities about

---

[2] Khosa, Mandla. "'Poverty Suicide Pact' Leaves Mpumalanga Mother, Niece Dead." Times Live, 30 Oct. 2015, www.timeslive.co.za/local/2015/10/30/Poverty-suicide-pact-leaves-Mpumalanga-mother-niece-dead. Accessed 7 Nov. 2015.

their difficulties instead of resorting to suicide." Just for the avoidance of doubt, South Africa is acknowledged to be one of the most unequal places on the planet.

There is further evidence: 800 to 900 miners die in mine accidents in South Africa every year. Historically, hundreds of thousands of others have contracted TB and silicosis and been sent home to die. The historical land question is proving hard to resolve, the housing backlog gets longer every year, shacks are a permanent form of housing for millions for whom hunger, violence, disease and malnutrition are a common denominator, and joblessness, unemployment, and underemployment are a constant national problem. There are no extant statistics of how many millions have historically been limited, and today are being limited, to being nothing else but domestic workers and gardeners. But we can be sure it is millions, and today we can add to that figure "car guards" and those young and old who live by rummaging in bins and carting trash for re-sell and recycling. Cases of racism trend in the media with increasing frequency. Surplus youths clog the townships and rural areas. So-called service delivery protests contribute to the picture of South Africa as the "protest capital of the world" (Duncan 2017). The government's solution to this Crime Scene? The minimum wage.

I have composed this keynote for *blackbodies*. The true nature of their password-exempt reality is not known in full or on its own terms. Instead, it is always known through deficit, in the light of what *infinites* and *finites* think, and in light of allocative tensions. I hope to change this. I have written this keynote partly in order to cut through the nonsense of the *finites* and *infinites* and to expose the evil *password projects* of apartheid that are found in every society and in every country in the world. The study begins in South Africa, where the most salient password project took shape from 1652 before disappearing constitutionally in the mid-1990s. I hope that this keynote can be a first step in reversing much of the harm done to the world by global password-modernity. Time is overdue when we should privilege and utilize, properly, the under theorized positionalities and corpora of ordinary men, women, and the youth who lived and continue to live under the loss of passwords. We need to understand how the modern world is organized on the basis of such *allocative loss*, so that we can undo this harm.

Apartheid, as far as it describes and explains the systematic allocation or exemption of passwords of being human, ultimately operates a dark operation at the heart of our modern times based on *algorithmically* covering up what is really going on in any given situation or context. That is, apartheid covers up global crime scenes. Apartheid Studies thus defines apartheid and shows how it operates, and in the process seeks to set up a new field of forensic studies. The forensic study of global crime scenes throws all of modernity into relief, such that we are able, firstly, to see how password regimes and algorithms shape our everyday lives *precisely*, and, secondly, to explain the true nature and maintenance of the so-called wealth of nations. The simple purpose of Apartheid Studies is to furnish types of empirical proof for the existence of apartheid that can pass muster in an argument or in a court of law, such that we are ultimately *assisted* to see, name, and root out apartheid. This task of *forensic assistance* is the task of Apartheid Studies.

III

Apartheid means *apartness*: but what does this *mean*? Historians and commentators have made the unforgivable mistake of regarding apartheid merely as a quantity or hardware – as something that is visible and quantifiable, like a house along a street or an ulcer on an elbow. This preoccupation with hardware leads us into an inevitable methodological *cul-de-sac*, where we see apartheid only through its signs such as pass books, Sharpeville, Soweto 1976, or obscene signs saying, "Whites only/Europeans only." Due to this blind spot, we fail to see much of the *quality* of apartheid. Pass books, signs saying "Europeans only," or the events of 1960 and June 1976, are *not* themselves apartheid. They are, instead, merely the clinical trials—the rehearsals—of apartheid. The clinical trial, in as far as it is an experiment, is not important in and of itself. Its importance, rather, lies precisely in the data and new knowledge it generates. It is all a *test*. It was always ever a test. This data and new knowledge are precisely what apartheid needs in order to get better and smarter at what it does. We must remember that apartheid, like any system, hates to be outmoded. It requires, rather, to adapt and move with the times. That is, any system that cannot find a permanent solution regarding longevity will cease to exist. The picture we are progressively revealing here is of an apartheid that learns from its mistakes and from its experiments. Essentially, in treating of apartheid, we must not fixate too much on the outward signs: these are not important in and of themselves. Sharpeville, pass books, and Soweto, seen outside the quality of data and new knowledge they generated, are meaningless. But if we regard apartheid through the prism of rehearsal, data, information, and knowledge, we see that apartheid is not in the past at all. Rather, apartheid is always adapting and evolving and has by no means reached its highest stage.

Apartheid means *apartness*, but what does that mean? The answer is that apartheid is *apartness* not so much in the sense of *keeping things apart* as in *telling things apart*. Apartheid is not mere apartness. Rather, it is transitive: it involves *telling* what must be kept apart. The crucial question is: how do you tell? True, the quantity of apartheid is commonly seen in distinct acts of keeping things apart. It is these acts that we, unfortunately, remember and exclusively associate with apartheid. But beating someone on the head with a police baton or lobbing a teargas canister into a crowded place is not *exactly* apartheid. Without generating data and new knowledge, without the crucial signal processing and information processing, beating up a person or causing them severe eye and respiratory pain through tear gas are mere accidents which anyone anywhere can cause. The truth is that any system predicated on *keeping people apart* requires, in the first instance, the use of a robust and precise means of *telling people apart*. Beating someone on the head with a baton requires that the policemen *be sure* that they are beating *the right person* i.e., that they are beating the person they are *meant* to be beating. Without this being able to *tell*, one cannot beat up another person. The policeman is paralyzed. The soldier's trigger finger freezes if he cannot identify foe from friend. The U.S. names its missile Hellfire on the assumption that someone else, somewhere, will experience the hellfire. No one designs missiles and names them Hellfire in anticipation of experiencing the hellfire himself or herself. The system has to be designed to wreak havoc *elsewhere*. AGM-114 Hellfire is named to reflect its design: that it must spit hellfire on Afghanis and Iraqis and Somalis, but not on U.S. citizens. But *how* does Hellfire know this? How does it learn its precision? Where does it get its extremely sophisticated targeting system? Where do "smart" weapons learn their smartness? Once we start asking these questions, we are already doing Apartheid Studies. We need to understand how a person is *meant* to be beaten, to breathe tear gas, to receive hellfire, or to be in the right place in a kill zone. A massacre or a genocide cannot even happen in the absence of a reliable *means of identifying* those exempted from exemption. Something *beyond reasonable doubt*, something tried and tested, must mark those who must suffer or die—else one will unleash a crisis that cannot be called back. The requirement of *precision* is all-important because failure to baton charge or tear-gas or shoot the right person throws the whole system into crisis.

To get a sense of what we are talking about, imagine the amount and level of crisis possible had the Angel of Death in Exodus 11 murdered the wrong first-born sons and *passed over* the *right ones*! The act of *passing over* (exempting from death) is meaningless without the act of *stopping over* (exempting the exemption) to dispatch those who are to die. That is, one passes over precisely *because* one stops over. But you cannot pass over or stop over in the absence of reliable information and knowledge. The centerpiece of the data was the bloodied door post. That is, the whole first-born thing hinged on *telling apart*. But, back to our line of inquiry: how does one *tell apart* those who deserve a beating from those who must not even be scratched? You can already tell that beating up a person is not half as important as *ascertaining* whom to beat up. The actual act of beating up Rodney King was not as important as the fact that the police beat up the right person. The distinction is a higher order, abstract thing. It would have been a crisis, in fact, had Rodney King not been brutalized. That is, there is always a latent crisis when the police *pass-over* a *stop-over*, in the same way that a crisis is caused by *stopping-over* a *pass-over*. The distinction between *pass-over* and *stop-over* is always grasped at deeper levels, as *discrimination*: something marked by the ability to see or make fine distinctions. To *discriminate* in this sense is to tell apart, foregrounded in a heightened sensitivity to precision. Thus, the important aspect of apartheid is *discrimination*. A beating is meaningless if it does not contain the key ingredient of discrimination. When meted on the wrong person, a beating is not only meaningless; it may mark the beginning point of revolution, particularly if it exposes a void, a weak point, in the system. Keeping people apart is not the most important part. True apartheid is in the recognition, in the software, in the algorithm: it feeds insatiably on the data generated by our daily lives.

Thus, anyone who means to keep people apart must, in the first instance, devise means to prevent their permanent mixing. The most primitive way of doing this is racial segregation. However, history has shown that racial segregation is never a permanent solution. If pursued too long and too rigidly, it becomes absurd and unworkable and falls into disuse. This is because race is unstable; it makes no sense to build a system on so unstable and changeable a thing as race. The real purpose of racial segregation is to experiment, to teach permanent lessons. Whereas racial segregation *itself* always gets abolished sooner or later, the lessons learned, and the data and new knowledge it generates about the capacities and limits of human beings, cannot be erased or abolished. Such data remains alive, available for use in contexts that have nothing to do with race, or where the outward signs and histories of racism have long been erased. This, I would say, is the difference between *keeping things apart* (KPA) and *telling things apart* (TPA). Keeping things apart is a surface level, low order, and uncoordinated set of *accidents* which anyone can set in motion. One cannot find true apartheid at this level. Telling things apart, on the other hand, is a deep level, high order, and step-by-step process which relates to the world of human beings through the prism of clinical trials and progressive revelation, and which generates *precision*. Without precision there is no apartheid. There is no apartheid if you cannot *tell things apart*, if you cannot *discriminate*, and if you cannot *pass-over* and *stop-over*. Apartheid, as a higher order means of telling things apart, is largely invisible[3] and ineffable and cannot be fully exposed except through an equally deep level, high order, and step-by-step process. This process of exposing apartheid is Apartheid Studies.

Keeping apart	Telling apart
Hardware-oriented	Algorithmic
Intuitive	Precise
Deterministic	Stochastic
Short-lived	Iterative
Infrequent	Frequent
Quantitative	Qualitative
Surface level	Deeper level
Lower order	Higher order
Mechanical	Abstract
Visible	Invisible

IV

Apartheid occurs across the world,

---

[3] Essentially, when we say that apartheid is invisible or that it has disappeared, we do not mean to indicate that it is not there. Apartheid is *always there,* and we mean to prove its existence. When we say that apartheid is invisible, we mean only to say that apartheid is *hidden in plain sight* (HIPS). Normally, people hide by keeping out of sight. They do this in two ways: by being as distant as possible from the seeker, or by installing themselves behind an obscuring quantity or mass. This traditional form of hiding we can call *hiding behind things*. HIPS, on the other hand, is something else: a higher level or higher order type of hiding which takes place *in front* of things. That is, it does not hide behind physical quantities but behind qualities: it is qualitative. Fundamentally, we do not mean to treat the very lack of evidence as evidence; we quite understand that the problem with saying that things are invisible is that this cannot be logically disproved—it can neither be proved nor refuted.

wherever there are human beings. It is not difficult to transition from Mpumalanga to the sweatshops of Bangladesh; in the collapse of the Rana Plaza in 2013; in the Grenfell Tower holocaust of 2017; in the Special Economic Zones of China; in the favelas and barrios of South America; in Yazoo City, Mississippi; in Downtown Eastside Vancouver; in the Roma slum of Stolipinovo in Bulgaria; in Rinkeby, Stockholm; in the invisibility of Polish migrants across Europe; the invisibility of Aborigines of Australia and Canada, and the permanent theft of their land; in Dharavi, Mumbai; Kibera, Kenya; and so on. There is no doubt in my mind that apartheid is a global paradigm.

Certainly, it is not such a large step from Mpumalanga to Warwickshire, England. In 2011, in Warwickshire, the bodies of Mark and Helen Mullins were found lying side by side at their run-down home. Although police described the deaths as "unexplained," *BBC News* describes the couple as "vulnerable."[4] It appears that they had decided to kill themselves rather than live impossible lives: they were tired of living "on very little," fighting "tooth and nail every step of the way," and walking 12 miles every week to a soup kitchen. Some months before their bodies were found, Mark Mullins had appeared in a video where he stated clearly that they were "caught in a catch 22 situation." He mused that they were in this impossible situation because institutions "just put a tick in a box and they alter your life."[5] How, though, does a tick in a box have the power to alter a whole human life? It appears that officials had decided, for instance, that Helen Mullins could not be employed as she had "no brain functions," numeracy, or literacy skills. At the same time, her incapacity benefits had been suspended due to the official reluctance to recognize her incapacity or diagnose her disability. "I think the system is very unkind," said Mark Mullins. Anyhow, following newspaper reports of the Mullins' "poverty suicide," Warwickshire Police confirmed that post-mortem examinations had "been conducted on the bodies of a man and a woman which were found at an address in Henson Road, Bedworth, on Thursday, 4 November. The results are inconclusive, and police are now waiting for toxicology tests to establish how the two people died" ("Inquiry," *BBC News*). Furthermore, the police were "not looking for anyone else in connection with the deaths, which are treated as unexplained at this time" ("Inquiry," *BBC News*).

Apartheid Studies thus seeks to define apartheid *anew*, in relation to the disappeared crime scenes and the neglected archive that surrounds us. In this new definition, apartheid is seen for what it truly is: a complex worldly phenomenon that is of significant interest to our attempts to understand the present and the future, to

---

[4] "Inquiry Call over Mark and Helen Mullins Deaths." *BBC News,* 9 Nov. 2011, www.bbc.com/news/uk-england-coventry-warwickshire-15645206. Accessed 5 June 2015.

[5] Good, Alastair. (2011-11-09). "Poverty Suicide Couple Had Warned of Hopeless Situation." *The Telegraph,* www.telegraph.co.uk/news/uknews/8878543/Poverty-suicide-couple-had-warned-of-hopeless-situation.html. Accessed 5 June 2015.

understand what is really going on, and to understand global modernity and the causes of the wealth of nations. There is scope to see how apartheid disappears and renders itself invisible, normal, and commonplace, and how it mutates, persists, and adapts to opportunities. Central to the design of apartheid is *metamorphosis*: it incorporates lessons learned, necessarily evolves with time, and adapts to changing environments and circumstances. Apartheid innovates and moves with the times.

Apartheid, it seems, does not seek to kill the human body outright, but merely to allow it to adapt to inhuman conditions. That is, apartheid puts human beings through inhuman tests, knowing that the human body adapts, short-term and long-term, to apartheid. These adaptations allow the human being to partially compensate for the absence of life that characterizes apartheid. Blackbodies are human beings who adapt and acclimatize to extreme inhumanity: they seem to have extreme tolerance and an infinite capacity for suffering. It is this capacity which modernity harnesses and depends on. Modernity, from this perspective is a dead zone and death zone. A dead zone is a part of the ocean that is so polluted that no life is expected to exist there due to lack of oxygen. That is, dead zones are areas of the seafloor with too little oxygen for most marine life. The "death zone," on the other hand, is a phrase used by some to refer to altitudes above 8,000 meters (26,000 ft.) where human bodies are said to reach the limit of their capacity to acclimatize. It seems that humans are not built to survive in such zones.[6] Those who survive in such dead zones, "death zones," and zones of non-being, become blackbodies. Adaptations always reflect much longer histories of living with apartheid. Even the deaths of blackbodies always represent significantly lower mortality rates because in fact more should be dying—since no one ought to be alive in dead zones anyway. It should not be possible to breathe, to sleep, to digest food, or to raise a family in dead zones. These are no places for human beings to live. And yet, against all reason and against all science, there are people who live there, who breathe, sleep, digest food, and raise families in dead zones. People in these zones live in a permanent austerity, where they have little choice but to redefine what is essential and what is not.

I am fascinated by the notions of *dead zones* and *death zones* precisely because human life, wherever it is found on earth, is demarcated and ringed around by such zones. For instance, although no one should live in poverty, billions of people *inevitably* do. And the sky does not fall just because billions live in poverty. No child should go to bed hungry. We know that. However, billions *commonly* do. And, still, the sky *does not* fall. No human being should eat food that has been thrown away. Yet many, many of us routinely live this way. No human being *should be without* a home. However, homelessness is a permanent sight across the globe. A contraption made out of cardboard,

---

[6] The concept of the death zone first appears in a 1953 article on acclimatisation by Edouard Wyss-Dunant.

tarpaulin, and plastic is neither a house nor a home. Yet, many hundreds of millions call such things home. Indeed, hundreds of millions know no other home. Does the sky fall? It is understood that people should not be segregated or discriminated against because of their genetic make-up: the colour of their skin, shape of their bodies, their gender, disability, and so on. However, people are *inevitably* segregated and discriminated against because of the colour of their skin, shape of their bodies, their gender, and level of ability. People have a right to clean, adequate water to drink, we are told. Yet many do not. Every human being has a right to justice, and yet billions *inevitably* live in injustice. Staple foods are *inevitably* eaten that some people, or their dogs, would not be seen eating. Minimum wages are *inevitably* paid out by people whose children would not accept such amounts for their weekly pocket money. *Inevitably*, prisons are proposed and designed by people who *themselves* never imagine spending any time in the kinds of prisons they propose and design. It is always *others* who must live their lives inside those metal bars and small spaces. Old clothes are donated by people who would *themselves* no longer be seen wearing such old clothes. Low cost housing is gazetted by people who would not themselves be seen sleeping in such a house. Job cuts are habitually proposed by people who *themselves* are certain that they will always have a job. Rubber bullet, teargas and live ammunition are fired at crowds of protesters by people who *themselves* would consider being fired upon to be a crime. Wage cuts are proposed and advocated by people who see no reason why *themselves* they should not take a bonus at the end of the year. People see no problem with sweatshops even though they, or their children, would never be seen working in such places themselves.

All these are examples of dead zones: zones of password *exemption* and *inevitability*; states of *inhabited inhabitability*. Our fascination is with these password-deprived chosen people who breathe in air that would *otherwise* be suffocating. That is, a dead zone is a black box: *somehow*, there is life in that lifeless place. How is it that there is life in a dead zone? It seems that it is a sort of miracle: that a person can be surrounded by so much hopelessness and disease, permanently live on such little food, drink so much unclean water, subsist on such low wages, live with so much harm and injustice, exist in the midst of such levels of crime and such crime scenes, and so on. It seems a sort of miracle that between the 1440s and the 1860s millions of human beings were traded, auctioned, and set to work, or that there was colonialism and empire. It is a miracle that there are sweatshops and export processing zones, open air prisons such as Gaza, and children dying in shack fires by the dozen every year in South Africa. The holocaust of Grenfell Tower in 2017 is a miracle of this kind, as is the shooting down of miners at Lonmin in 2012, and the collapse of Rana Plaza in Bangladesh in 2013. Singapore, South Korea, Hong Kong, and Taiwan—the so-called Four Asian Tigers (or Four Asian Dragons or Four Little Dragons) which underwent rapid industrialization, maintained exceptionally high growth rates in excess of 7 percent a year, and developed into high-income economies—seem to be miracles of this kind.

But these are not so much miracles as states and circuits of apartheid, or circuits of the *occult*. Special Economic Zones are *special*, it would seem, precisely because they constitute *occultic* zones *set aside* by governments, in connivance with corporations, in order to signal that we are now entering dead zones where "normal" safeguards need not apply. That is, the "special" in Special Economic Zones means *password exemption*: a place where the *being* of some humans is loosened, put in abeyance, or rendered inoperative. The *free* of Free Trade Zones, Free Economic Zones, Free Economic Territories and Free Zones refers, on the other hand, to the complex alchemy that allows the World Trade Organization (WTO), for instance, to institute an Agreement on Subsidies and Countervailing Measures for purposes of umpiring and maintaining—rather than abolishing— the world's occultic zones.[7] The freedom lies in the *precision* with which dead zones are *set aside* – so precise that voices of protest are muted and *life goes on*. After all, we have not seen the sky fall because a country sets up and operates Special Economic Zones. Rather, *ceteris paribus*, developing countries are "opened up" for business, and there is expectation of rapid industrialization and high growth rates. The job of the WTO, in that case, is to keep the sky from falling. *Ceteris paribus*.

In the dead zones of the world, life is deliberately held in abeyance. Singapore, South Korea, Hong Kong, and Taiwan underwent rapid industrialization and maintained *exceptionally high* growth rates precisely *because* of the circuits of the occult. China has been doing the same thing since the 1980s and continues apace. The occult is a powerful thing: China has even declared an entire province, Hainan, to be a Special Economic Zone. Dozens of countries across the world are falling over each other to follow suit.[8] What is going on? The answer: competitive advantage. One commentator on the World Bank blog observes, "Why did the African zones fail, in the past, to attract many investors? My answer was they were not truly 'special' in terms of business environment and infrastructure provisions, and many constraints were not significantly improved inside the zones" (Fruman). The idea, it seems, is to properly leverage a country's store of dead zones: the nature and *availability* of dead zones in a country attracts capital and economic growth.

---

[7] Says the WTO:
> The WTO Agreement on Subsidies and Countervailing Measures disciplines the use of subsidies, and it regulates the actions countries can take to counter the effects of subsidies. Under the agreement, a country can use the WTO's dispute-settlement procedure to seek the withdrawal of the subsidy or the removal of its adverse effects. Or the country can launch its own investigation and ultimately charge extra duty ("countervailing duty") on subsidized imports that are found to be hurting domestic producers.

"Subsidies and Countervailing Measures." *World Trade Organization*, www.wto.org/english/tratop_e/scm_e/scm_e.htm. Accessed 13 August 2018.

[8] Fruman, Cecile, and Douglas Zhihua Zeng. "How to Make Zones Work Better in Africa?" *The World Bank*, 27 July 2015, blogs.worldbank.org/psd/how-make-zones-work-better-africa. Accessed 14 August 2018.

Dead zones—who would have thought—are the hubs of competitiveness. The occult is a powerful thing: the World Bank says dead zones must be *truly special* in order to attract more investors. That is, dead zones will work *if and only if* they are *truly* dead! *The occult is a powerful thing*: Africa has a lot to learn from China, where an entire province has been declared a dead zone. The stakes are heightened: apartheid is being demanded in broad daylight. Out of the dead zones of the world, therefore, comes the *wealth of nations*. It could be said in the future that one may recognize the density of apartheid in the world by the availability of "free" and "special" economic zones.

At any rate, all these are examples that generally demonstrate one crucial thing: modernity is founded on and underwritten by very precise *circuits of the occult*. It is the purpose of this keynote address to suggest how these circuits function and how the *wealth of nations* is *caused* and *maintained*. We said dead zones are sites where "normal" rules and safeguards are inoperative. But what is behind the *suspension* and *countervailing* of "normal" rules? What causes it? How is the "normal" itself negotiated? How is the normal countervailed? What is behind this special form of *exemption*? How does *password exemption* work? How do we recognize it when we see it? Apartheid Studies seeks to answer these questions.

Dead zones thus constitute veritable *states of password exemption*: people exist where normally they would be extinct. Daffodils emerge out of concrete. Life sprouts from that which has a default setting set to annihilate life. Life exists out of lifelessness itself. *Abusus non tollit usum*.[9] In the world there are, therefore, two non-complementary zones: the world, and its dead zone. The two are non-complementary in the sense that one exists *within* the sacrifice of the other. The one dies so that the other lives off the corpse's compost or fills up the vacated space. The one is the mill, and the other exists to be fed into the mill. That is, modernity is an *algorithm*, much like breathing in and out. The world takes in oxygen, in order to live, and breathes out *inevitably* unwanted waste in the form of carbon dioxide. The abstraction of oxygen, and the exhalation of carbon dioxide, results in a dead zone. That is, dead zones are the dump sites, landfills, recycle spots, and sewage works of the world. Without them the world lives in filth and sooner or later chokes to death. This two-zoned world, its reproduction of ineffable crime scenes, its *states of inhabited inhabitability*, of *inevitability*, and the *state of password exemption*, is what we call *apartheid*, because it is predicated on respiratory algorithms for *setting apart large numbers* of sacrificial chosen ones who routinely suffer in the world's innumerable dead zones; *large numbers* who tighten their belts and are conditioned to hypoxia and anoxic austerity; who, like so many mutating Christs, persistently die *so that* others live; who are diseased in *large numbers* on behalf of a healthy world; who eat what others discard, and generally *carry the costs* and burdens of living.

Modernity functions primarily as the *eye of a needle*, through which password-exempt, austerity-adapting

---

[9] Latin for "Abuse does not preclude use."

chosen people have to pass. That eye of the needle is, in fact, an algorithm: *apartheid*. These chosen ones are the *hata* of the world, the caryatids, the cartilages, and the shock absorbers.[10] In this paper, we call them *blackbodies* because they are *perpetually available* to *perfectly absorb* shocks, crises, risks, scandals, losses, and blows. Blackbodies are modernity's *insurance scheme*. In this way, all the good things come out of the dead zones of the world. Out of the dead zones comes the *wealth of nations*. The study of dead zones, black boxes, blackbodies and the wealth of nations is Apartheid Studies.

It is, of course, not always obvious to everyone that modernity and its triumphs, from stock exchanges to skyscrapers, high speed trains to holiday resorts, micro-chips to self-driven cars, are invoiced and levied on dead zones and blackbodies. It will seem hard to some to credit dead zones with producing the wealth of nations—as hard as attributing billions of dollars of the wealth of the modern world to the trade in human beings that started in 1441 and ended in 1834. On what basis should the attribution be possible? After all, the appetizing yumminess of grilled steak and chops often bears little relation to the stomach-turning smells, blood-spattered walls, death-tinged atmosphere, deathly moans, and gruesome violence, of an abattoir. Yet, there will not be any mouth-watering steak and chops *without* the grisly abattoir. Thank God for the abattoir! Such death zones as abattoirs are responsible for the precious protein and delectable cuisine enjoyed in faraway restaurants. Out of grisliness and foul smells comes succulence and lusciousness. *Abusus non tollit usum*.

The relationship between the restaurant and the abattoir is therefore wholly *algorithmic*, in that the steak and chop is *invisibly parasitic* on the abattoir, like the fungus that hijacks the reflexes of the carpenter ant in the rainforests of Brazil. Basically, the tastefulness of the steak is directly proportional to the indiscernibility of the sickening noises, violence and smells from the abattoir. The taxation takes place in a black box. The further the violence of the abattoir is disconnected from the restaurant menu, the tastier the steak and chops. That is, to understand how blackbodies are the wealth of nations, how they perfectly absorb crises, risks and blows, and how costs are passed on to them, one must think of the notion of *indirect taxation*. Costs are passed on invisibly down the supply chain. To be a blackbody is therefore to be *invisibly taxed*, as by an *invisible hand*. Forget what Adam Smith said: the true invisible hand is the *algorithmic allocation* of costs and burdens, as in a black box, onto blackbodies. It is like removing the black-and-yellow do-not-cross police tape from a crime

---

[10] Shona word for any substance used to *absorb* shock. Women drawing water from the well or finding firewood from the forest or mountain-side, for example, would construct a *temporary*, round, padded, cushioning object from *any available* soft material such as cloth, bits of grass or leaves, to put on their heads so as to protect their skulls from the weight and discomfort of the load they will be carrying. The purpose of the *hata* was thus to absorb pain, discomfort or shock. The material for *hata* was expected to be readily *available* whenever needed and to be *discarded* or set aside (for other purposes) after use. *Hata* were thus immensely useful but also immensely disposable.

scene. The crime scene disappears with the police tape. But has it really disappeared? No, the crime scene is still there. However, it is now enclosed in a black box. Peer as you might, you will not see anything, even with a magnifying glass.

Apartheid Studies, in this sense, is a new, deeper forensics that attempts to see crime despite the absence of the police tape. We now know that the invisible hand is the black box within which burdens and costs are "harmlessly" invoiced, levied, billed, taxed, transferred, and *teleported* onto blackbodies. We know this because there is no trace in the figures of the trades of the Johannesburg Stock Exchanges (JSE) of the dust, heat, silicosis, tuberculosis, and rock falls that are the lot of the gold miners underground in coffin-like shafts. That is, the stomach-turning smells of the abattoir are, magically, *no more* in the steak and chops. The invisible hand—the algorithm—has noiselessly, losslessly, and autonomously *filtered* them out. The skin lacerating leaves of sugar cane from the plantation leave no traces in the bowl of sugar that goes into the breakfast cup of tea. The chocolate bar has none of the bitterness of the sweat of children laboring on cocoa farms in Ghana. The "white" city *invisibly taxes* the township. All the cleanliness of the shaded streets of the northern suburbs of Johannesburg is directly proportional to, and parasitic on, the uncollected rubbish in the township of Alexandra. Notice when Fanon (1963) talks of the native town and the colonizer's town.[11] The relationship between the colonizer's town and the native's town is one of indirect, algorithmic, parasitic tax. The profits on the Johannesburg Stock Exchange are directly proportional to—*parasitic on*—the number of retrenched blackbodies: cost cutting, cost control, and cost saving. Out of retrenched black bodies came value traded in cash equities market, up 13% year on year in the first half. At least, this is what the business websites are saying:

> *The JSE's turnaround plan seems to be working.*
>
> The bourse's holding

---

[11] Fanon, Frantz. *The Wretched of the Earth*. Translated by Constance Farrington, Grove Press, 1963.

> The settlers' town is a strongly built town, all made of stone and steel. It is a brightly lit town; the streets are covered with asphalt, and the garbage cans swallow all the leavings, unseen, unknown and hardly thought about. The settler's feet are never visible, except perhaps in the sea; but there you're never close enough to see them. His feet are protected by strong shoes although the streets of his town are clean and even, with no holes or stones. The settler's town is a well-fed town there, an easygoing town; its belly is always full of good things. The settlers' town is a town of white people, of foreigners.
>
> The town belonging to the colonized people, or at least the native town, the Negro village, the medina, the reservation, is a place of ill fame, peopled by men of evil repute. They are born, it matters little where or how; they die there, it matters not where, nor how. It is a world without spaciousness; men live there on top of each other, and their huts are built one on top of the other. The native town is a hungry town, starved of bread, of meat, of shoes, of coal, of light. The native town is a crouching village, a town on its knees, a town wallowing in the mire. It is a town of niggers and dirty Arabs. (38-39)

company—JSE Ltd, which *cut 60 jobs in a scramble to reduce costs*—said in a trading update on Tuesday that its 2018 half-year earnings were *expected* to be a *vast improvement* on the same period in 2017.

Last year was disastrous for the exchange, which, like many South African companies, was battered by lackluster economic growth and political uncertainty.

The JSE felt the pinch through reduced trading revenue, as jittery investors reluctant to take big bets on companies' fortunes knocked total value traded on the JSE by 13% year on year in the first six months of 2017.

The JSE has furthermore had to contend with the first challenge to its monopoly in 60 years with the launch of four new stock exchanges in SA over the past 18 months.

The most threatening of these, A2X Markets, is providing a secondary trading venue for JSE-listed stocks at reduced trading costs. While A2X and its peers have yet to gain traction, *the JSE has responded* to the competition by announcing a new *billing model*, effective at the end of July, which will lower trading costs.

The JSE further responded to the changing competitive and economic environment by retrenching 14% of its workforce in 2017 to save R100m in the 2018 financial year. The bourse also cut spend on technology, removed vacancies and reduced discretionary spend.

Cost cuts and *increased revenue* were the *major reasons for profit growth* in the first six months of 2018, said Harry Botha, an analyst at Avior Capital Markets. Value traded in the JSE's cash *equities* market, its *mainstay*, was *up* 13% year on year in the first half, Botha said. [....]

The *expected increase* in headline earnings per share to 638.2c-687.3c was *largely due* to "*cost control*, a once-off taxation credit of R31m as well as *growth in revenue*," the bourse said.

The tax credit related to an investment the JSE had made about five or six years ago to update its legacy broker dealer accounting system. In the end the system had not been replaced, Botha said.

He was forecasting *20% earnings growth for the full year on stronger revenue.*[12]

Cost control means stronger revenue. It is blackbodies that constitute stronger revenue: 14% retrenched = R100 million *savings* in the first half of 2018. 14% retrenched = 13% year on year in the first half. This algorithm works this way because the stock exchange does not know or care where blackbodies go after retrenchment, or what they eat, or whether the children have school fees or school uniforms, or rent has been paid. *Earnings growth* does not know the size or shape of a shack, or the

---

[12] Ziady, Hanna. "JSE Upbeat over Result of Cost-Cutting." *Business Day*, 18 July 2018, www.businesslive.co.za/bd/companies/20 18-07-18-jse-upbeat-over-result-of-cost-cutting/. Accessed 18 July 2018.

materials used to construct it: cardboard, tarpaulin, copper wire, rusty nails, discarded tins, and so on. The *bourse* (the purse) does not know malnutrition, or a rumbling stomach. Rather, it cares about the total value traded and about jittery investors reluctant to take big bets. The bourse is also feels really *threatened* by secondary trading venues and *billing models*.

Apartheid Studies is meant to show the links: the abattoir in the steak and chop, and the steak and chop in the abattoir; the slum in the suburb, the suburb in the slum; the retrenched blackbodies in the bourse, the bourse in the retrenched workers, and so on. Apartheid Studies is thus an equation: 14% retrenched = R100 million *savings*. When you are able to smell (and hear) abattoirs on your dinner plates, you have Apartheid Studies. The blood that stains restaurant menus, stock exchanges, skyscrapers, billing models, high speed trains, earnings growth, holiday resorts, IPOs, investor confidence, micro-chips, retrenchments, cost control, the Internet of Things, and self-driven cars must become altogether visible and readable. Apartheid Studies in this sense is simply an attempt to define the wealth of nations *properly*. To the study of black boxes, dead zones, and blackbodies we add *billing models*.

V

In a South African film from the early 1990s, *There is a Zulu on my Stoep*, a farm worker goes into the bush to defecate. The man stoops and commences his excremental business. Unbeknownst to him, however, two boys are intent on pranking him: they unobtrusively slide a shovel under the man's bums, quietly drag away his excrement and tip toe away with to hide in the bushes some distance away. The poor man, upon finishing his business, rises to wipe his bums, only to discover that his excrement has disappeared. Where has the excrement gone? The failure to see his feces nearly drives him out of his senses. He even checks the pockets and sleeves of his overalls but finds nothing.

There is a lesson here: it is not possible that there can be no excrement. *There is always excrement*. Though we cannot see it, we know it is there. Like the poor farm worker, our concern is: where has the poop gone? Where has the excrement of the fabulous skyscrapers, the stock exchanges, the World Economic Forum, Disneyland, ritzy hotels, and palatial suburbs disappeared to? Modernity disorients so much because it hides its excrement. Capitalist modernity has reached the heights it has due to disappearing its poo within circuits of the occult. Apartheid Studies is the attempt to locate this poo—to locate these vanishing circuits of the occult and vanishing crime scenes.

Blackbodies circulate within these vanished *circuits of the occult*. What do I mean by this? Circuits of the occult are those instances in which the inheritance of the bodies that do the actual suffering and that absorb blows, mortality, risks, and crises on behalf of those that accrue the credit *has been erased*. The notion of the *occult* is used here to mean that a kind of transformative magic is going on: the names of *those who are carried* across crocodile infested rivers are memorialized, while those on whose shoulders they perched are forgotten.

Those who were carried across hippo-infested rivers are called "explorers." The *carriers* are not named. No one bothers with that. Possibly, it is considered a waste of names. I say that it is *occultic* when people who never spent a day underground in a gold mine and never held a drill in their hands *carry off* all the profits and royalties, while those who descend *into the depths* five days per week—to face rock falls, earthquakes, dust, silicosis, tuberculosis, and brain-frying temperatures—are *inevitably* allotted a minimum wage or are massacred by the police when they go on strike to demand a raise. Those who receive the gold ore on the surface and pawn it on the commodities exchange are *inevitably* memorialized as the "gold miners" and the Randlords. The sky does not fall.

A famous example of the *occultic* is the inscription on the "explorer" David Livingstone's tomb in Westminster Abbey. The inscription is occultic because it only remembers the name of David Livingstone. He is the missionary, traveler, and philanthropist. He has a resting place. *Inevitably*, those who carried him across crocodile infested rivers are denied the fame of the travelling they did, the missions they went on, and the philanthropy they did. Instead, it is Livingstone who travelled, went on missions, and did philanthropy. His words are remembered and memorialized. A clue to the nature and function of the occultic are the opening words of the inscription: "Brought by *faithful hands...*" (emphasis added). The blackbodies that did the *bringing* are *inevitably* remembered only as *body parts*, never as persons with names or a full humanity and identity. Chuma and Susi are only hands. The hands are only noticed because of what they brought: Livingstone's corpse. They are *bringing hands*: it is whom they bring that exempts them from the exemption, from the complete invisibility and total erasure of the dead zone. *Inevitably*, body parts themselves have no value: they only bring value. Thus, there is a town in Zambia called Livingstone. There are innumerable schools and streets named after Livingstone. Yet there is not a single town, street, or school named after Chuma or Susi. Who names towns, schools, and streets after body parts? You will never find Chuma and Susi's names or faces memorialized on coins or bank notes. And yet, it is because of Chuma and Susi that Livingstone rests in Westminster.

Chuma and Susi, meanwhile, do not rest: their resting place is not known or memorialized. Body parts do not rest. After all, they are merely instruments for conveying value. Blackbodies are conveyor belts: conveyor belts do not own what they convey. They also do not complain. After all, it is their job to convey. *Inevitably*, their business is *merely* to convey. What else are they good for? Chuma and Susi's traveling, mission-work, and philanthropy is thus not known: for they did not do any traveling, mission-work, or philanthropy. They merely *conveyed* Livingstone from place to place, like wagons. Chuma and Susi came to attention *only* because they *conveyed* Livingstone's corpse for thousands of miles and accompanied it to England. Their value is *inevitably* in conveyance. Chuma and Susi came to attention *only* because they were a pair of servants. Whatever they were, whatever they did, is known *inevitably* by accident: because of Livingstone. Chuma and Susi can *only* be known *through* Livingstone. Without him they *inevitably* fade into nothing. Without his corpse on their shoulders, they do not exist. Their traveling, carrying, mission-work, and philanthropy only exist as a faint echo in Livingstone's journals. No famous, living words are attributed to them. It is as if they said nothing. Conveyor belts do not talk. It is as if their whole lives boiled down to a golden destination: destined to convey Livingstone's corpse to the coast. If you take away Livingstone's corpse, you have no need for conveyance—hence, you have no more need for Chuma and Susi. They instantly disappear.

Chuma and Susi enter the historical record only *because* they were devoted, loyal, and faithful body parts. They exit it as they entered it: devoted, loyal, and faithful body parts. Is it not interesting that Chuma and Susi are only known as Chuma and Susi, as a couple, never as individuals? That is, they exist only as far as the spectrum of the poles they use to hoist Livingstone's corpse: they are known only from the opposite ends of the funerary hammock resting on their shoulders. Chuma and Susi's descendants inherit no such "rest." Indeed, it is not known if Chuma and Susi have any descendants. Who cares? Were Chuma and Susi first names or surnames? No one cares. They probably came from present day Mozambique or Malawi, but who cares? It is not known where their lives ended or how. No one cares. It is Livingstone that is important.

The circuit of the occult is the reason Chuma and Susi do not "rest" to this day. It is the reason their resting places are *inevitably* not known. It is the reason for a famous image of Livingstone *carried across* a river. In his journals, Livingstone never says that it was his nameless servants who crossed the river with him clinging on their shoulders. Instead, *it was he who crossed the river*. How is this possible? How can a person cross a river while sitting down—except when he or she is perfectly conveyed by a machine? How can you claim to have walked from point A to point B when you were being carried from point A to point B? How can you walk while being carried? Who walks while being carried? Who walks on another's shoulders?

What kind of walking is this? And yet, this is *exactly* the kind of crossing and journeying that *inevitably* gives Livingstone his fame as a traveler. Livingstone's journeys are all stolen from his *footsore* servants. What did Livingstone really do *as Livingstone* to make him be the only one that is known and memorialized far and wide today, despite the train of servants that conveyed him from place to place? How is it that, despite the fact that it was impossible for Livingstone to achieve anything without his wealth of burden-bearing servants, it is only Livingstone who rests in Westminster Abbey? Where are Chuma and Susi? The servants made Livingstone possible, but where are they? Who remembers? Who cares? All these puzzles and questions confirm the Livingstone paradox: walking while being conveyed. It is this form of "walking" that explains the circuits of the occult upon which modernity is built.

If one looks at the picture below, it is clear that none of the faces of these burden bearers is visible so that one can put a name on it. Only Livingstone's face is legible. He is the only person in the picture. The others are merely body parts: hands and feet. None of the blackbodies in the image have a known resting place or fame as travelers, missionaries, or philanthropists. Yet, they did all the actual *body-guarding*, the eternal fending off, risking life and limb, doing all the carrying, burden-bearing, travelling, and the missions for which Livingstone is famous for.

Circuits of the occult thus express the theft of wealth: they function to snatch body parts from their owners,

name today: they were merely hands and feet, *body parts*. Those that stayed on the surface and dealt on the stock exchange owned those body parts through the cost of capital. This is the Livingstone paradox, the circuit of the occult, and the wealth of nations.

The deep subterfuge of the circuits of the occult is aptly expressed in the occultic idea of the white man's burden.[13] Magic, we all know, is the opposite of reality. The reality is that blackbodies, trapped in dead zones, are the true wealth of nations. Rudyard Kipling, of course, is correct in his proposition that modernity is constituted as a burden. However, he

DAVID LIVINGSTONE, SUFFERING FROM FEVER, CARRIED ABOVE WATER ON THE SHOULDERS OF ONE OF HIS MEN. WOOD ENGRAVING AFTER J.B. ZWECKER, 1814-1876. WELLCOME COLLECTION IMAGE NO. 5614421. CC BY 4.0.

and to use those parts as if they had no owners, or as if the owner was the person being blithely conveyed along. The wealth of the gold mines of Johannesburg, for instance, supposedly, *inevitably*, belongs to those who never carried a shovel, hammer, or a drill, and who never descended into the bowels of the earth to meet stifling heat, dust, silicosis, tuberculosis, earthquakes, rock falls, or winch accidents. Those that went into the ground are not remembered by

gets his wires crossed in terms *who carries whom*. What Kipling imagines to be the white man's burden is, in fact, merely a burden of guilt, arising from the hoarding of stolen wealth from such occultic events as the slave trade, colonialism, and empire. The Livingstone paradox shows who actually waits in the harness and does all the carrying. The burden of guilt expresses itself as the master's wish for the permanent, occultic disappearance of reality.

---

[13] Kipling, Rudyard. "The White Man's Burden." *Internet Modern History Sourcebook*, sourcebooks.fordham.edu/mod/kipling.asp. Accessed 16 June 2017.

VI

I have always been impressed, since childhood, by the Biblical account of the ten plagues, and the deaths visited on the first-born sons.[14] What interests me in particular is the fact that the plagues and the deaths are *selectively allocated* and *apportioned*: plague and death are allotted in such a way that those who suffer plague and death, merely by suffering plague and death, effectively *immunise* others from plague or death. Thank God for *hata*, or blackbodies. It was clear that there was an *algorithm* at work. The plague-and-death seems to know *when* and *where* to STOP to cause destruction, and *when* and *where* to *pass* so as not to cause destruction. As I read the parable, I thought that there seemed to be a kind of reference book at work, a kind of pass book, or automated balance sheet, which the plague and the Angel of Death checked, re-checked, and reconciled in order to make sure when to START or STOP. As we know, every good algorithm has to know when to START and STOP. It is not an algorithm that does not know how where or when to START and STOP.

What has always fascinated me is the *allocation* of death and plague. How does such *apportionment* and *allocability* work? How does something *selectively allocate* and *ration out* plague and death to some and not to others? What sort of *work* is this? How are those who are to suffer *chosen*? It is clear that plague and death are a function of a universal *algorithm* that recognizes and allocates plague and death, dead zones, and plague zones. Essentially, those who are plagued and who die are not only chosen—that is, *sacrificed*—in this special role but are chosen on the basis of a singular *algorithmic formula*. That is, some are diseased and deceased SO THAT others are not diseased and deceased. It is this that has always struck me: the *algorithmic function*. Put another way, the *sacrificial function* in modernity is *algorithmic*. The plagues and death are *passed on* like a baton is passed on. Everything happens in a *step by step* way. That is, rather than everyone being diseased, only some are diseased *instead*. Instead of everyone dying, *only some* die. Already there is an *algorithm* clearly at work: some, not others. Algorithms, of course, work *inevitably*. Likewise, apartheid.

The carrying of burdens is, we saw earlier, an act of *password exemption*. No one can accept a minimum wage, a meal from a dust bin, or a home under a bridge, unless they enter a *state of exemption*. I find that the state of password exemption is fully and completely *algorithmic*: it *chooses, allocates,* and *rations* those whom it affects. Blackbodies are in this sense the chosen people. So far, we do know *why* blackbodies are chosen: because the sky will not fall. Earth will still circle the sun. What we do not know for sure, however, is *how* these algorithms work, how *password exemption* works. We do not know *how* blackbodies are chosen. One popular explanation for apartheid is racial: that those who are chosen for exemption are chosen *because* of their race. Hence in South Africa apartheid is synonymous with racial segregation. However, this explanation, despite its popularity and

---

[14] The sequence of plagues begins with the bloodied Nile, followed by infestations of frogs, lice, flies, livestock deaths, boils, hail, locusts, darkness and, finally, death of first-born (Exodus 7:14 to Exodus 12:36).

currency, is demonstrably weak if we accept that apartheid operates on the basis of algorithms. Algorithms are unable to recognize race, since race is a myth and a construct. That is, algorithms only accept logical *sequences* and *parameters*—otherwise they would not know which steps to follow, what input to read, or where to START or STOP. The absurdity of defining apartheid by reference to racial segregation is shown by such farcicalities as the pencil test, the one-drop rule, eugenics, craniology, nose measurements, and the so-called bell curve. Algorithms cannot understand or admit such mumbo jumbo. The case of Sandra Laing, at any rate, blew racial explanations out of the water by proving beyond all doubt that such explanations were lazy, pseudoscientific, and could not stand a robust test. That is, claims of racial superiority are impossible to uphold with any consistency. To defend such claims, one has to speak almost out of the arse.

The racial explanation definitively crumbles the moment we admit racial *admixture* (so-called coloreds, mulattoes, Creoles, quadroons, and so on): How are coloreds a race? How are they not a race? Are they or are they not? How is it possible to persist in attempting to definitively distinguish between black and white *if* it is proven that so-called black and white can and do *mix*? What race is it that is half-black or half-white? Where does one belong who is three quarters black, or three fifths white, one eighth black, four sevenths white, five sixths black, two thirds white, four ninths black, and so on? The racial explanation, from this angle, seems patently absurd as an explanation for apartheid. Even white racists everywhere seem to know this—as illustrated by their generalized phobia of miscegenation. Racists fear miscegenation precisely because they understand that racial mixing gradually strips away the myth of the immutability of race and exposes the flimsiness of race as an explanation for why things are the way they are in the world. Any racist who claims to be superior but fears miscegenation, contradicts himself.

The distribution of plague and death in the book of Exodus helps us see that password exemption works *algorithmically*: you die, SO THAT others live (like some kind of Jesus Christ). You are diseased, SO THAT others can stay pure. That is, plague and death are already factored in, not only *so that* specific people START to be diseased or to die, but plague and death STOP when they reach a certain *threshold* or *watershed*. Whatever burden you carry is not only being carried *on behalf* of others, but the sky will certainly not fall because of the allocation of your burdens. I have written *Apartheid Studies* mainly in the hope that it can illuminate the question of *how* apartheid works. This for me is the crucial question. We know, so far, that its algorithms specifically *choose* their "victims," according to some threshold or *sustainable* watershed. But we do not know *how* the algorithms choose, *how* they know what is sustainable or is not, or *how* (or *when*) a threshold or healthy watershed has been reached. We know that the algorithms know when to START and STOP. However, we need deeper study and further thought and analysis to understand *how* the algorithms know when to STOP and START. The Egyptians were certainly *not* chosen for death or plague because of their race, as this would be apocryphal. The concept of race, as we know, is a fairly recent construct. But, even if we admit that race might have been a factor in the *selection* and *allocation* of plague and death, such an explanation breaks down if we consider that the Angel of Death that killed the Egyptian first-born sons *had no idea* how to distinguish Egyptian first-born sons from Israelite first-born sons – hence the strict instruction to Israelites to specifically *mark* their doorposts.

That is, the Angel of Death did not *pass over* Jewish households by looking at the race of those it was to kill. Rather, it chose an easily recognizable and truly *algorithmic* parameter: a bloodied door post. If you are going to kill *so many*, with such lethal *precision*, race is useless as a parameter. Had the Angel of Death sought to use race—whatever race is—to select and allocate those it had to kill, it is probable that many Jews would also have been caught in the cross fire. We know that in the Rwandan genocide, many Hutus, who looked like Tutsis were supposed to look, were killed by the *Interahamwe*. It is not possible to tell a Hutu from a Tutsi visually unless one believes the discredited Hamitic myth. It is not possible to remain a pure Tutsi precisely because there are no pure Tutsi (or pure Hutu) to begin with. The futility of preventing miscegenation exposes the inanity of those who imagine that they could somehow remain pure. The Angel of Death in Exodus 12, therefore, could only have carried out the genocide of first-born sons by using something *automatable*, almost machine readable and constituting a kind of database. Apartheid, it seems, works with the *law of large numbers*. Those it chooses must be found in large enough numbers to assure immunity for those on whose behalf they suffer—a sort of economy of scale.

There are three crucial questions that can be posed in relation to the *algorithmic* nature of apartheid. The first is that once the algorithms had started beyond the first step, the crucial question of *precision* arises. How do the algorithms know *when* and *where* to STOP? That is, how did the Angel of Death know *when* and *where* to stop its killing of the first-born sons of Egypt? How is death distributed, *parsed*, controlled? What unique *data* does it draw on? The second question is about *immunity*. We were rightly puzzled about *scalability*: how the Angel manages to *parse* death and *pass over* those it is under strict *instruction* to spare. But what is the exact *nature* of this *parsing* and *passage*? What relation does the Angel's *guarantee* of immunity and *exemption* of immunity have with South Africa's notorious *pass* laws? The last point is about *sustainability*. How did the Lord know *how much* plague was *enough*? *Precision, immunity,* and *sustainability* are central to the notion of apartheid, and we shall briefly touch on this centrality.

On the question of *precision*, we hear that, "The houses of the Egyptians shall be full of swarms of flies, and also the ground on which they stand. And in that day I will *set apart* the land of Goshen, in which My people dwell, THAT no swarms of flies shall be there" (Exodus 8: 20-22, emphasis added).[15] Whenever I have reflected on the distribution of plague and death in our modern times, I have always thought about the *setting apart* of the land of Goshen. Precision here is not a mere question of geography: the land of Goshen is not merely *set apart* in physical terms so "that no swarms of flies shall be there." Rather, it is an *instance* and a *state* of being *reserved, out of reach*, like a virtual machine. I began this keynote by saying that human beings are not substances and *hence* cannot be put into a test tube. To make the houses of the Egyptians, and the very ground on which they stand, be full of swarms of flies, while *simultaneously* setting apart the land of Goshen in *such a way* that no swarms of flies shall be there requires nothing less than an aptitude for *experimenting* with humans. This is what the Lord is doing: he is carrying out an experiment. Experiments, as we know, have only one purpose: to see or show what happens. You *intentionally* manipulate substances or surroundings in order to see or show how things *behave* under certain conditions. The land of Goshen is the Lord's control arm. He uses it *precisely* to demonstrate the principle of *immunity*: the state in which things were before the swarm of flies.

Precision is important, otherwise God would never know for sure if the supposed effects of the plagues were being produced *only* by the plagues themselves. For instance, for the swarms of flies to be attributed solely to God, it was necessary that there be no other competing swarms. The swarm of flies had to be the only swarm of flies in Egypt at the time. *Control* is integral to the whole thing: God could not claim that he was the one behind the plagues if he could not control the variables. If he could not control the variables, he could not claim to be the one behind the suffering of the Egyptians. Precision, therefore, was necessary in order to demonstrate a statistically systematic change in the Egyptians *due* to the plague.

The parable of the land of Goshen illustrates for us that apartheid is intrinsically *parasitic*. That is, it essentially arises out of an obsession with *precision*. Hey there, look at me: I come out of plagues unscathed. Behold, the deaths of others are no concern of mine. I am warm in the frostbite. The homelessness around me is not my fault. Come, now, poverty is everywhere, is it not? The problem is *over*population, suggested Malthus. To understand *how* the concept of *precision* lies at the heart of apartheid, we need to consider how Goshen remains *untouched* in the midst of the plagues. Precision concerns how the plague *moves about* in Egypt *in such a way* that it leaves Goshen untouched. How does the Lord *move* the plague about with *such* precision? What are the plague's specific *instructions*? This ought to be our interest: the instructions. What has the plague been told to do? We know that the plague afflicts some and misses others. How it does so we do not know. Apartheid Studies in one sense is about determining how plagues know. How are plagues controlled and managed? How do plagues learn? How is *precision*

---

[15] *The Bible*. New King James Version, Thomas Nelson Publishers, 1975.

achieved?

Immunity presents the same core problems as precision. We know that *immunity* is a function of afflicted bodies: by the mere fact of being afflicted, Egyptian bodies *absorb* the plague into themselves and shorten its *reach* and lifespan.[16] The reason the plague does not *reach* the land of Goshen is *precisely* because it has all but been snuffed out. That is, by the mere fact of being located *outside* of Goshen, one *attracts* the plague as if one were a magnet, and one's body is turned into a *hata* or a buffer. A buffer is defined as a cushion-like device that *reduces shock* due to an impact. It can also refer to an inclined metal frame, placed *at the front* of a locomotive, to *clear* the track of obstacles. We have heard about buffer zones: structures that act to absorb and interrupt risk before it spreads:

> Throughout the whole length of the spine, the vertebra are bound together by strong fibrous bands or ligaments, but *between* the body of each vertebra, there is *placed* a *pad* or *disc* of *cartilage* or *gristle*. These discs are *elastic* and allow a slight amount of movement *between the bodies*, and also act as *shock-absorbers*. They *diminish the jolt of blows* upon the head, or *falls* upon the lower end of the spine, or upon the feet (9, emphasis added).[17]

This bears restatement: zones of cartilage, or gristle, *diminish the jolt of blows*. These *gristly* zones, as we will see, not only play a critical role in apartheid but constitute the wealth of nations.

We did say that it was important for God to be *certain* that the supposed effects of the plagues were produced *only* by the plagues themselves. The Lord's integrity is at issue here. For instance, the swarms of flies could not be fully or solely attributed to the Lord if it were discovered that a swarm of flies had been seen in a certain part of Egypt a few days before Aaron stretched his hand in order to begin the seventh plague. Hence the Lord's swarm of flies had to be the *only* swarm of flies in Egypt at that particular time. He had to *control* the variables. By *setting apart* the land of Goshen, or by killing only the first-born Egyptian sons, the Lord is taking care to eliminate alternate explanations for the order of things. That is, the true value of the land of Goshen lies in its power to *cause* apartheid: harm is caused to others *without* cost to oneself. Apartheid cannot happen *if* there are *confounding factors*. This is the sense in which all the ten plagues of Egypt are *stage managed* templates of apartheid: the plagues produced results as expected. That is, the ten plagues are fake news of a kind because *none* of them constitute a *true* crisis. Take, for example, the death of the first-born sons of Egypt: this event—regarded as the most important plague of all resulting in Pharaoh giving in at last and hence marking the beginning of the exodus—is not a true crisis at all *precisely* because the Lord planned, expected, and induced it. To eliminate all confounding factors and to ensure that he got all the credit, the Lord would have had to make sure that no first-born Egyptian sons died before

---

[16] I am reminded of the labels on some medicine bottles: "Keep out of reach of children."

[17] South African Red Cross Society. *Manual of First Aid*. 1954. Cape Town: Galvin and Sales, 1983.

the allotted time or died from an accident, illness, or some other natural cause.

A *true* crisis, however, does not work this way. Rather, a true crisis, by definition, is impossible to prepare against: it upsets the balance of order, confounds all allocative algorithms, and ensures that things will no longer be the same again. Events such as Soweto 1976, #RhodesMustFall in 2015, and #FeesMustFall in 2016, for instance, count as true crises. In Exodus, a true crisis would have been *if*, for some reason, the Angel of Death had fallen sick and not been able to carry out his task, or if he had developed stage fright or eyesight problems leading him to massacre those he had been instructed to spare and spare those he had come to kill. Only this kind of accident constitutes a true crisis. Had the Angel killed the first-born sons of Israel instead of the first-born sons of Egypt, the Lord's experiment would not only have been thrown into disarray but would have been *exposed*. The blood on the doorposts, or the land of Goshen, thus act as scientific controls of a kind: they are there to mark the *immunity* from the plagues, in order to ensure that the balance of order is not eternally upset, and apartheid's *black box* is not exposed. The state of affairs at Goshen must remain *stable* and *the same* at all times *throughout* the plague. This is the sense in which apartheid is a long-acting, chronic state.

All the work of apartheid, thus, is bound up with *crisis*: there must be no crisis. Rather, every crisis must be precisely, perfectly, absolutely, intuitively, and inevitably *absorbed* by blackbodies. That is, the algorithm of apartheid *defines* precisely, perfectly, absolutely, intuitively, and inevitably where safety is to be found (that is, in Goshen). How does it do so? It does so through *reserving* the crisis precisely, perfectly, absolutely, intuitively, and inevitably to those places that are *not* Goshen. Think how the Glen Grey Act of 1894 and the 1913 Land Act created in South Africa the *reserves* into which the "natives" were to be *confined* and *locked-in*. Think, for a moment, how Sir George Grey drove AmaXhosa, and Sir Theophilus Shepstone the AmaZulu, into "locations" in the mid-1800s. Observe how indigenous people in the United States, Australia, and Canada were herded into *reservations*. The purpose of Cecil Rhodes' Glen Grey Act, the 1913 Land Act, the locations in the Eastern Cape and in KwaZulu-Natal, and the reservations in the United States, Australia, and Canada, was to *reserve* the crisis, *precisely*.

The paradox-laden question of *reservation* is complex and occupies a critical place in Apartheid Studies. We mentioned above that there are two non-complementary zones in the world: the world and its dead zone. The two, we said, are non-complementary in the sense that one exists *within* the sacrifice of the other. That is, the one dies so that the other lives off the corpse's compost or fills up the vacated space. The one is the mill, and the other exists to be fed into the mill. The notion of reservation is one way of demonstrating how the separations of apartheid work. Through the construct of *reservation,* we are able to observe how, for instance, parasitic Europeans arrive in an assumed *terra nullius* and soon *enclose* their African hosts in a "commons" (so-called reserves), while, in fact, *reserving* for themselves perpetual and open access rights *outside* the enclosure they create for Africans. Reserving land for the exclusive use of Africans within the cage of the reserves, locations, and townships is a ruse that plays two roles. Firstly, it is meant to *free* whites to appropriate whatever else is not inside the cage. Secondly, it is a form of sustainable colonialism or sustainable development in that it grants the African some land instead of taking all of it away. Of course, the land allocated and granted to Africans is, in reality, a prison. Hence, the purpose of reservations into which blackbodies are herded is precisely to *reserve* the rest of the land for the *exclusive* use of whites. That is, the imprisoning of blackbodies functions to free parasitic Europeans to claim whatever lies beyond the gates of the prison. As such, two "commons" are created. First is the commons of the colonized, which is located inside of a prison. Inside the prison commons the blackbody is "free" to do anything that he or she wants as long as he or she stays inside and does not leave without permission or a pass. The second commons is that which is created out of the creation of the prison-corner of the African commons: the white man's or colonizer's commons. The white commons are anything that becomes available due to the herding of blackbodies into their prison-commons. In other words, the colonizer's commons are the rest of the country, the rest of the land, and literally all the wealth since there is no ownership in prison. The concept of *reservation* is crucial in Apartheid Studies because it demonstrates how and why parasitic whites have a tendency to take, and take, and take.

Whereas in the prison commons, where blackbodies are sent to be "free," the world stops, the rest of the world becomes the white man's playground: his exclusive commons with open access rights. This is the meaning of the apartheid phrase "developing along their own lines." It means that the world is divided into two fake commons that specifically and precisely facilitate exploitation and the rape and theft of wealth and land.

The link between Goshen and *reservation* is hard to miss. By *reserving* the crisis, the apartheid algorithm not only precisely and inevitably *allocates* the plague but also *ensures* that there is, in fact, no crisis. The creation of *reserves*, whether in South Africa, Australia, Canada, or in the United States, has never been an *accident*: the act of *reservation* is always intentional. That is, the algorithm of apartheid works like an *insurance* scheme. How does it do so? By ensuring that the crisis, because it is *confined*, turns out not to be a crisis. That is, the algorithm literally *insures* Goshen: it *insures* land invading Europeans in the United States, South Africa, Canada, and Australia. By *allocating* the swarm of flies precisely, perfectly, absolutely, intuitively, and inevitably, the algorithm *ensures* that the crisis is *friendly*. At least, no crisis that is confined to blackbodies can be construed to be hostile. Here, a contemplation of certain considerations of fire insurance might allow us to evaluate, in passing, how such hostility and friendliness operates. An issue of the *Yale Law Journal*, for instance, has considered that "the test of a 'hostile' fire is that it be *accidental* and burn in *a place not intended*" (emphasis added).[18] In one case, *Pappadakis v. Netherlands Fire & Life Insurance Company* (1926), a fire was held to be hostile because it *escaped* through a crack in the oven. In *Samuels v. Continental Insurance Company* (1892), a flame was held to be hostile because it flared up *two or three feet above* the lamp chimney. In *Hansen v. LeMars Mutual Insurance* (1922), the burners of an oil stove turned up *too high*, causing the stove to give off smoke and soot. Our infernal algorithm, it seems, *insures* against hostility precisely by ensuring that crises are *friendly* (that is, they burn only in *places intended*). That is, apartheid ensures friendliness! It is not an accident that H. F. Verwoerd, the Nasionale Party prime minister whom some historians and commentators regard as the father of apartheid, defined apartheid as a policy of "good neighbourliness." Blackbodies make "good" neighbors precisely because they absorb modernity's crises in such a way that such crises reach neither Verwoerd nor Goshen.

At issue, therefore, is the *locus* of the fire: Goshen *is* the *place not intended*; Verwoerd and the Europeans settled in South Africa, the United States, Canada, and Australia regard themselves to be the *persons not intended*. The rest of Egypt, on the other hand, is a *place intended*. Blackbodies in South Africa and across the world are *persons intended* for they satisfy the law of large numbers: they are poor in *large numbers*, are shot at in *large numbers* by soldiers and police, are diseased in *large numbers*, live in slums in *large numbers*, suffer in *large numbers*, are enslaved in *large numbers*, provide cheap labor in *large numbers*, are evicted in *large numbers*, and die in *large numbers*. This, it seems, is the right moment to think hard about the ten clinical trials of Exodus. Had the Lord, in the seventh clinical trial of Exodus, failed to allocate the swarms in *such a way* that they went *only* to *places and persons intended*, then we would have had a proper crisis on our hands. A crisis, therefore, is when the plague spills into Goshen. A crisis occurs when harm happens to *persons not intended*. This is what the *Yale Law Journal* calls an accident: when the swarms meant for Egypt *escape* through a crack in the wall, when a flame flares up two or three feet *above* the lamp chimney, and when the burners of an oil stove turn up *too high*.

In the case of *Lavitt v. Hartford County Mutual Fire Insurance Company* (1927), judgment was given for the defendant because "[t]he evidence showed that the fire was *at no time outside of* the furnace" (emphasis added). The phrase "at no time outside of" is speaking about *precision*. It was held, in the *Lavitt v. Hartford County Mutual Fire Insurance Company* case, on appeal, that "the judgment be affirmed on the ground that damage by smoke and soot from *a fire confined within the furnace* was not covered by the policy" (emphasis added). Hence, there is no crisis *so long as* there is *confinement*; so long as the crisis is *confined* precisely, perfectly, absolutely, intuitively, and inevitably, there is no crisis. Rather, there is nullification. That is, there is *inevitability*. Essentially, it is only those things that escape *confinement* that are held to be hostile. A crisis, however excessive or not expected, is not a

---

[18] "Insurance. Fire Insurance. Damage from Smoke and Soot of 'Friendly Fire.'" *The Yale Law Journal*, vol. 37, no. 2, 1927, pp. 264-265.

crisis as long as it is confined to defined borders and boundaries. Good neighbors are those that stay confined. Hostile neighbors, on the other hand, bring about a crisis for apartheid. In the case of *O'Connor v. Queen Insurance Company* (1909), it was found that the fire, though confined to the furnace, burned with unexpected violence and excessive heat. Though confined, the fire burned, as we saw, with unexpected violence and excessive heat in the Bambatha uprising of 1905, at Sharpeville in 1960, in Soweto in June 1976, at Lonmin platinum mine in 2012, with #RhodesMustFall in 2015, and with #FeesMustFall in 2016. Hence, "The first court called upon to construe the meaning of fire in an insurance policy denied recovery for damage done by smoke on the ground that the fire was of ordinary size and confined to a furnace."

We will see that blackbodies are the signal, constitutional reason there has not been a single true crisis in the world since the dawn of modernity in the 15th century when the first transatlantic slave voyage set sail for Portugal in 1441. For a crisis to happen, blackbodies will have to be *unavailable*. That is, they would have to stop being tolerant to extreme conditions of the dead zones. Basically, the basis for blackbodies' extreme tolerance within capitalist modernity is their surreal ability to absorb blows, tighten belts, adapt to austerity, tolerate abuse, and live with injustice. Essentially, this means that blackbodies are able to discriminate among different contexts and environments. For instance, one knows not to trespass in certain places. Blackbodies know, for instance, to fight other blackbodies in the township, slum, and favela rather than fight true extremophobes who live in the safety of the leafy suburbs and gated communities. They also do not typically invade private property or rob banks. Rather, they invade each other's spaces and rob other poor people. In this way, they pump out the social order and reproduce compatibility which maintain the equilibrium of modernity and the wealth of nations.

There is no crisis *precisely* because Goshen creates a kind of reaction matrix: the crisis is contained within specific borders or bodies. We know from chemistry class that one cannot merely add water in order to convert sulphur trioxide to sulphuric acid, else the reaction is *so uncontrollable* (exothermic) that it creates an acidic mist, vapor, or fog of sulphuric acid. To avoid the fog of sulphuric acid, the sulphur trioxide is first dissolved in concentrated sulphuric acid.[19] Blackbodies are controlled precisely in order to avoid exothermic bursts of activity that spill beyond dead zones. Crime waves must be restricted to townships. There must be no house breaking in the leafy suburbs. That is, the key to the function of the apartheid algorithm is the *endothermic* process: the blackbody *absorbs* crises, instead of *releasing* them. In terms of the reaction matrix, only *some* people will ever die or get diseased at a given time in a given

---

[19] Sulphur trioxide dissolved in concentrated sulphuric acid yields the following:

$$H_2SO_{4\,(l)} + SO_{3\,(g)} \rightarrow H_2S_2O_{7\,(l)}$$

That is, dissolving sulphur trioxide in concentrated sulphuric acid results in a product called fuming sulphuric acid, or oleum. It is oleum which is then reacted *safely* with water, to produce doubled quantities of concentrated sulphuric acid.

$$H_2S_2O_{7\,(l)} + H_2O \rightarrow 2H_2SO_{4\,(l)}$$

place. The reaction matrix is thus arranged algorithmically, optimally, to enable a safe, stable and efficient genocide of the first-born of Egypt. There is little chance that the genocide will spread to the first-born sons of Israel. It seems that it is necessary to be *precise* in handling and dealing with a crisis perhaps because, as scientists say, the absolute amount of energy in a given state is difficult—if not impossible—to measure or calculate precisely. Hence the crisis must be endothermic. Ultimately, we are faced with a surreal paradox: it is because *munhu munhu*—because human beings cannot be reduced to substances—that apartheid seeks to reduce them to substances.

Apartheid thus concerns the development of a reaction matrix that reproduces borders and blackbodies within which modernity's crises can be contained and safely set off. How can danger interact *safely* and *inevitably* with safety, death *safely* and *inevitably* with life, wealth *safely* and *inevitably* with poverty? How can perturbation not perturb? That is, how can risk, death, danger, and crisis be directed, managed, channeled and localized? How, indeed, can densities of death and disease be made to be profitable? How do we *correct* for death and disease? How can townships coexist side-by-side, *safely,* and *inevitably* with leafy suburbs? How does one correct for poverty, so that it is *inoperative* in some places? That is, how is poverty to exist *independently* of riches and wealth? We know this is possible because the world is full of islands of wealth surrounded by seas of poverty. If you can make poor people in townships and rich people in leafy suburbs *coexist* and orbit *together*—that is, if life can go on—then you have apartheid. It is all about dealing with a *microarray* of respective *densities* and their corrections: high densities, medium densities, and low densities. The density of water, we know, is approximately 1g/mL whether you consider a drop of water or a swimming pool. High densities of death in Africa, low densities of death in America, but life must go on. High densities of death amongst black people in police shootings, low densities of death amongst whites, but life must go on. Densities of HIV are recognized as being higher in Africa, or in black communities in America, and so on.

We hear about what are called key populations: blackbodies. Again, densities. That is, blackbodies carry dead zones with them wherever they go. They absorb crises as a rule: this remains true regardless of 'quantities' of blackbodies that are in or are not in a given place at a given time. That is, blackbodies still die and suffer in *large numbers* regardless, whether it is televised or not. It does not matter whether no one knows about it, whether it happens in Brazil or Palestine, Shanghai or the Democratic Republic of the Congo. It is the same algorithm. What we called the law of large numbers and the law of *persons intended* is at work, regardless. There can be no other explanation. How does a bomb go off, as it did in Hiroshima and Nagasaki, *precisely* in the place where it is meant to explode so that it will kill *only* those persons it is *intended* to kill? How does a bomb *intend*? How does a bomb know? Do bombs know? Do bombs know whom they kill? Do viruses intend? How do they know whom to infect *in large numbers*? How does a bomb go off at the time it is meant to go off, in the required way, with the required impact? Indeed, how does a bomb kill *safely*? I talk about a *microarray* because all these things are linked. A child dying of malnutrition in Ndjamena, Chad, is linked to the New York stock exchange; a boat of economic refugees capsizing in the Mediterranean is linked to the World Economic Forum. A township in South Africa is linked to a slum in Kenya. Tens of thousands of black men in prisons in America are linked to thousands of Aborigines in prison in Australia. It is a microarray of apartheids. The algorithm is one and the same.

We have covered *precision* and *immunity* and shall now touch on the third point, *sustainability*, which concerns how the Lord's algorithms know *how much* plague is *enough*. That is, though it seems certain that the algorithms of apartheid know *how* to START and STOP, we are not yet sure how they know *when* to START or STOP. Like *precision* and *immunity*, the question of *sustainability* is an issue of *control*. Things must not be in crisis. That is, a *true* crisis must be prevented at all costs. Whatever happens, the balance of order must not be upset. Hence, the plagues had to be *controlled*—not endless, yet not too brief; not countless dead, yet not too few dead either—in order to achieve the required behavior change. That is, apartheid is inherently *discriminative*. It chooses its victims carefully. It is seldom what it seems and never really stands still: it may go on along a certain path for as long as it has to, before abruptly changing direction. Apartheid changes form at will and *metamorphoses* to suit changing circumstances and conditions. It is always seeking to achieve more with less and adapts to fast-changing worlds. It can achieve multiple feats on each step of the algorithm, and it is scalable, interoperable, even customizable.

Ultimately, the deeper issue concerning *precision*, *immunity*, and *sustainability* is the unmistakable *interdependence* of Goshen and Egypt. Goshen is a living contradiction: it is like a part of the body that lives off its own dying body. How can a body part remain *un*infected when the rest of the body has HIV? How does Goshen remain *immune*? This *immunity*—this difference between Goshen and the rest of Egypt—is the ultimate puzzle of apartheid. Although the rest of the body weakens and suffers punishment (and eventual death), Goshen *separates* itself. How does the death of the host *not* endanger the parasite? How does death *know not to* endanger those that feed on the proceeds of dying?

Whenever we go back to *that* original charter of apartheid from the Book of Exodus, we learn four important things. The first discovery is about the algorithm. How we seek to explain the world, human relations, action, reaction, cause, effect, identities, modernity, and so on, is best done by reference to algorithms. Secondly, we learn that the fact that there existed an algorithm in Egypt that allocatively rationed out plague and death *is* the reason the sky will not fall. It is possible to know *why* there is apartheid. Thirdly, we learn that apartheid will not operate except on the basis of a kind of database, with *large numbers* of blackbodies. Perhaps this is the means by which the question of *threshold*, *watershed*, and *sustainability* is resolved. Finally, the question of how apartheid works is the most important one. Such a question, however, will not be settled by resorting unimaginatively to explaining apartheid through race. At any rate, racial segregation will not help us to understand *how* apartheid works—how it chooses its targets, and so on. To understand how apartheid works, we need to delve deeper.

I have, thus, always wondered about the nature of these *chosen ones* who carry plague and death so that others might live. These chosen people carry within themselves *immunity* or the wealth of nations. The original charter of apartheid of the ten plagues and the deaths of the first-born sons is, in fact, a scaled-up version of an older moment: Genesis 22. The ram with its horns conveniently caught in the thicket is *chosen* to absorb Abraham's dagger-blows *in place of* Isaac. The function of the ram is to literally *deflect* the blows of the dagger away from Isaac's body, so that they sink into its body instead. The miraculous presence of the ram thus *defuses* a dangerous crisis. The ram's trapped body, for some reason, is implicated in a very sordid business. No one, however, has ever bothered to ask what business the ram has dying *in place of* Isaac, or why the contract between God and Abraham should be inked with the ram's blood. Why should Isaac not die *in place of* Isaac?[20]

VII

Blackbodies enter and exit modernity *as* body parts. The fate of those body parts is to perpetually seek password protection, often by desperate means. The crux of the problem, as we saw, is apartheid: modernity functions as a sieve, an eye of the needle. It provides password protection only in exceptional cases. There are thus billions of Chumas and Susis in the world: body parts of the dead zone, queueing for passwords, waiting to pass through the eye of a needle. In May 2018, Mamadou Gassama, a Malian economic refugee in France, was fortuitously awarded the password of French citizenship and Paris' Grand Vermeil medal because *his body parts* had climbed an impossible four stories to save a child dangling from a window. Before that impossible act, Gassama had been just another blackbody in a dead zone: illegal, unwanted, and unknown. Before being invited to the Elysée Palace to be offered citizenship and a job in the fire brigade, Gassama had left Mali in 2013 as a 17-year-old teenager seeking to enter into Europe by crossing the Sahara Desert through Burkina Faso, Niger, and Libya and then traversing the Mediterranean to Italy. This was his uncertain journey to retrieve a password—a journey which often ends in death by drowning, internment, life in migrant camps, or a precarious existence as a "paperless" person. Like the millions of refugees in Europe seeking exemption from the dead zone, Gassama knew the risks of seeking such passwords: Europe only offers passwords in exceptional cases. Europe only offers *fortuitous passwords*. Gassama, like millions of others, was intercepted (at sea) by police on his first attempt.

On his second attempt in 2014, Gassama finally got to Europe. From

---

[20] Had the ram not shown up, then God would have been shown to be a liar for He had previously promised Abraham that Isaac's children will fill up the earth. The function of the sacrificial ram is thus a way for God to save face.

Italy he travelled to France. We know that had there been no cameras fortuitously present to capture Gassama's spider-man act, he would still be a resident of the dead zone: illegal, unwanted, and unknown. His life would still be lived in that dead zone like those of all other migrants. None of those who awarded Gassama a medal would have noticed or cared. It is hard to notice signs of life in the dead zone except in exceptional cases. After all, no one expects to find life in the dead zone. Passwords can only be exceptional. Modernity would collapse were large numbers of blackbodies to be given passwords from the dead zone. Hence blackbodies still have to pass through the eye of a needle. Even as Gassama was receiving the accolades in the city council room, the Parisian police were busy razing to the ground migrant camps just a few kilometers north. Millions of Gassamas will not be offered passwords from the dead zone unless their body parts do impossible feats that are fortunate to be noticed by those who may have the power to offer passwords to certain individuals from the dead zone on the basis of impossible feats *that are noticed*. Billions of body parts, Chumas and Susis, go unnoticed, and will not be fortuitously offered passwords that will enable them to exit their dead zones. Billions of hands and feet are fated to miss the eye of the needle.

VIII

The explosion of scholarship in Europe and North America on the subject of *austerity* since the 2008 financial crisis makes a sickening, grating sound in the ears of most people who subsist in the so-called Third World and on the peripheries of industrial society. The simple explanation for this reaction is that the lives of *sacrificial bodies*—blackbodies—from Africa, Asia, South America, and elsewhere have more or less been bound to an anoxic austerity since about the time Columbus landed in the so-called New World. The blackbody's experience of austerity is that of being permanently *kept alive*, as disposable live bait in a tank or black box, for the last six centuries. That is, blackbodies subsist as steps in an *algorithm*, marked by their perpetual availability to be *adjusted* and *cut* in order to correct for shortfalls, costs, expenses, losses, and deficits. When the gap between expenses and revenue is narrowing, the normal way to keep it open is by plugging in as many sacrificial bodies into the hole as possible. In this way, the risk of default is averted. This is the main sense in which blackbodies are the wealth of nations. They absorb risk. As long as the world maintains an adequate collection of blackbodies, life can go on as it has been going since the 1400s. The elites in Europe, the United States, Canada, Australia, and New Zealand who are moaning about austerity have no idea what austerity *really* is.

In order to properly understand the link between apartheid and *modernity*, I propose that we imagine *live bait* in a fisherman's tank. It is true that, in order to fish at all, the fisherman needs his bait. It is this bait that will bring the fish to the hook. However, the live bait itself is less important than the fish. Indeed, the live bait is kept alive only for the sake of catching the fish. That is, the live bait is never kept alive for its own sake. The whole point is the fish(ing). The *expenditure* on *maintaining* the live bait *cannot exceed* the *income* or *revenue* from selling the fish. In this little parable, I have just described what economists call a budget deficit. However, this parable does more than just express the mechanism of a deficit. Rather, in this parable I have attempted to spell out the whole saga of modernity. Modernity is the *austerity*, or *sacrifice*, or password exemption of *blackbodies*. Blackbodies, of course, are the *live bait* that constitute the *wealth of nations*. The means by which blackbodies are kept alive is called *apartheid*.

Modernity, after all, is a direct result of the multiple and permanent *austerities* that *define* blackbodies as the wealth of nations. All the moaning about lean times, cutting down, living within means and tightening belts, coming from Europe and America, is thus annoying and laughable: blackbodies are invented in the parent algorithms of austerity that made Europe and America possible in the first place—the transatlantic slave trade, colonialism, and empire. What makes the moaning of Europe and America egregious is that for a long, long time Europe and America have been largely *exempted* from the austerity visited on the rest of the world for the last six centuries. The permanent historical austerity visited on blackbodies was the source of this *password exemption*. The reason Europe and America are in deep crisis at this moment is precisely because significant breaches seem to be developing in historical *states of exemption*.

IX

Before I launch into my conclusion, I would like to reiterate that I think there is great value in understanding how our contemporary worlds *really* work. It seems fitting that anyone who exists in our present time should know something of the nature and scope of how modernity itself is *caused*, reproduced and *maintained*. I assert that the only true means to fully understand our modern times is to first appreciate—definitively—the true nature of what Adam Smith called the *wealth of nations*. Precisely, this address is about the *nature* and *maintenance* of that wealth. I believe, however, that we have been misled by the crude economism of the economists and those who agree with them that the *wealth of nations* is somehow to be transparently found within the seemingly rational workings of capitalism—gross national product, free trade, capital accumulation, macroeconomics, microeconomics, the free market, division of labor, supply, demand, foreign direct investment, the stock exchange, foreign currency, debt, credit, and so on. The truth, of course, is rather simpler and, perhaps, much more sinister. Capitalist modernity arises out of and is maintained by a simple innovation: the abolition of God.

How does one abolish God? First of all, we need to understand that God is merely a principle: the principle that *everything has a price*; that *everything exists at a cost*; that *there is no free lunch*. God is the Eternity of Cost: it is impossible to get something for nothing. This principle is built into and constrains every relation and every relationship of every being alive on earth. It is this principle, because of its *inescapability*, that establishes who or what God is. This truth is itself God, because it functions to limit and constrain the whole field of human action, ensuring that all human beings everywhere are equal, whoever they might be, whatever the circumstances or the time of day. By this principle, harms such as slavery, rape, theft, exploitation, oppression, injustice, racism, xenophobia, and genocide are found to be *ungodly*. To my mind, such a principle is more important than freedom, religious belief, law or democracy, because none of them would exist *anyway* without it. As I have said, *it is* God.

Now, if everything has a price, it means that even *profit*—capitalism's single greatest objective—naturally and necessarily comes *at a cost*. This is an important point because we know that in modernity profit is a super-religion: the supreme justice is the justice of profit, and everything that happens in our world happens in order to realign the balance of profitable forces. We know that books must be balanced, and that the *balance sheet* rules our lives. However, the claim that *everything* comes at a cost seems to contradict the very concept of a balance sheet. How is this the case? Basically, if profit *naturally comes at a cost*, it means that *profit itself*—the supreme order of modernity—not only can never be guaranteed but is progressively exposed to be *unattainable* and an *illusion* since wealth is perpetually being destroyed in the same moment and amount that it is created. *All things are always losing value.* In order to exist at all, things must give up value. Loss is value. Value is loss. Basically, if we followed God, there would be no profit, no savings, and no capitalism. Indeed God, framed this way, seems fairly and squarely anti-capitalist. The crucial question, therefore, is how capitalism exists. That is, how can it exist? How does capitalism exist *at all*? Indeed, how is there modernity? How are our modern times possible? What happened to God? What happened to everything having a cost?

It is true, capitalism rules our lives today. It is the new *inescapable*. We replicate its algorithms in the minutest details of our everyday lives. That is, capitalism is *too big to fail*. We cannot do without it. It is like oxygen. But how did this *systemic importance* of capitalism come about? How did it come to be unquestioned? The answer lies in the wealth of nations, but perhaps not in the way we conventionally think. For something to become the wealth of nations, it needs to be *invisible*, like oxygen. This is the sense in which Smith speaks of the invisible hand: something which moves us without our notice. We all know how we hardly notice oxygen. We pretty much only notice it when, for some reason, it is withdrawn, and we struggle to breathe. This is how important it is: it is so important that we do not notice its presence. For capitalism to become *as important as oxygen*, it needed an innovation so simple that no one would notice. It needed to be *exempt* from God.

Essentially, the only way to *guarantee* wealth—to guarantee that profit would not be lost every time it is made—is to abolish God. That is, it had to become possible to get something *as if* it were from nothing. Remember, we have said that God is basically the eternal cost, the unavoidable illusion. God is merely the complex expression of the fundamental and inescapable principle that:

1. there is no free lunch,

2. everything has a price,
3. things cannot be got from nothing,
4. therefore, everything comes at a cost.

Capitalism needed to violate this unavoidable rule that says that *all things have a cost*. It needed to avoid the unavoidable. As long as this rule persisted, it meant that *profit itself* was one of those things that naturally came at a price and was therefore, in actual fact, illusory and unattainable. Profit could not exist. Profit cannot exist. That is, profit cannot exist as long as God exists, because God is equilibrium: the expression of the illusion of profit. As long as this illusion exists, capitalism cannot exist. Essentially, God is the existence of *that which cannot exist*. This is the sense in which capitalism and God cannot coexist. Capitalism needs profit, not God. God has no use for capitalism. That is, capitalism needs that which cannot exist *to exist*.

Hence capitalism's greatest innovation is that it *even* exists at all. That capitalism even exists is what should properly astound us. This bears repeating: *capitalism cannot exist*. At least, it should not be existing. If there is God, there should not be capitalism. Does this mean that there is no God? Is capitalism proof that *God is not*? The existence of capitalism is extremely irrational and impossible, because it is predicated on making exist that which cannot exist: *capital*. To understand this, we need to understand the relation of capital, surplus value, profit, and suchlike. Profit is widely agreed to be the best measure of success in an enterprise. After all, it is the basis on which tax is computed, dividends are paid, and so on.

But what really is profit? We are told that profit is the *surplus remaining after total costs* have been *deducted* from total revenue. Now we need to keep our eye on those keywords: "surplus," "remaining," "after," "total costs," "deducted," and "total revenue." It is said that profit is reflected in reduction of liabilities, increase in assets, and/or increase in owners' equity. But how is *surplus* at all possible? How does profit *remain*? What is this thing that remains *after* total costs have been deducted? Is there an "after" *beyond* total costs? What does this "after" look like? What do we understand by *total costs* anyway? How are total costs *deducted*? Once again, we are reminded of the definition of profit: profit is *gain*, especially the *difference* between the amount earned and the amount spent. How, then, is capital at all possible? How can surplus value exist? Where does profit come from and where does it go?

If everything *always already has a cost* and there is no free lunch, *how is profit possible*? If it is impossible to get something for nothing, *then* how do we end up with capital? If everything has a price, what happens to *the price of surplus value*? Indeed, how can there be surplus value *at all* if cost is eternal? We know, from the God principle, that *costs are always there*. Costs are eternal and are not deductible. One cannot do without costs: costs are like oxygen or the four laws of thermodynamics. Because of the eternal cost of things, perpetual machines of the first kind cannot exist. And yet the likes Smith, Ricardo, Mill, Marx, Malthus, Hume, Keynes, Schumpeter, Hayek, Veblen, Friedman, von Mises, Pigou, Pareto, and the rest of the celebrated economists, all seem to think that capital is *an actual thing*. Since when has capital become an actual thing?

How can capital exist? How can capital exist with or without cost? How can capital exist *at all*? Indeed, there is no way capital can exist if the principle of the eternity of cost implies that costs are, like energy, *indestructible*. Costs can neither be created nor destroyed. Rather, they can only be *transformed* from one form to another. Le Chatelier's principle says that the *position of equilibrium* always moves in *such a way* as to tend to undo whatever change you have made. Profit, if we understand it as an act of *extraction* (which it is), means that the position of equilibrium will *always* move to replace whatever has been extracted. There is nowhere to hide. That is, there can be *no* cost-less or cost-free extraction. Cause and effect; act and reaction. *Nothing*, except the circuits of the occult, can be got from nothing. This takes us back to Chuma and Susi: the Chuma-and-Susi principle tells us that it is *not* possible for there ever to be *no costs*. Livingstone cannot walk and be carried at the same time. Forget it: it is *just* not possible that there can be no costs.

Costs are, then, the only *constant*. They are not deductible, and it is this *indeductibility* that makes *life itself* possible. The *position of equilibrium* is *always* on the move, from right to left, correcting for any deductions. The equilibrium constant will *constantly* move in such a way as to counteract profit's *extractive* attempt at cost-less deduction. Hence my line of questioning: how can one rationally claim to be able to *deduct* cost? Can Livingstone claim to have crossed a river when we know he did so perched on his servants' shoulders? We are talking here about what is possible and what is not. Anyone who thinks we can *deduct costs* is wasting time: it is a sleight of hand which has no effect whatsoever on cost. The *position of cost* is always on the move, always being transformed, but is never destroyed or deducted. I opened this chapter by saying that human beings are not substances: *munhu munhu*.

The *indeductibility of the human being* is at the heart of Apartheid Studies. Indeed, there is *no place to hide* from this principle, a fact which may explain why the innovation of the occult has been to hide in plain sight.

The simple proposition which I make and challenge the economists to refute is that *cost* is materially, rationally, objectively, and logically *indeductible*. To deduct cost is to abolish God. To deduct cost is to turn a human being into a test tube and human life into a clinical trial. Is that what capitalist modernity is? One may only deduct cost *in theory*, as part of a meaningless *technical* accounting exercise, but never *in practice*. Technically, Livingstone crossed hippopotamus infested rivers. Technically, Livingstone was a world-famous explorer. In reality, he was a fraud. That is, he literally *defrauded* those on whose shoulders he perched who are not credited with this *carrying* in the Livingstone diaries. In reality, Livingstone plagiarized the discoveries of *those who carried him*; he converted—embezzled—Chuma and Susi's bodies to his own personal advantage. In reality, *profit is not possible* because costs cannot be deducted. *Munhu munhu*. A human being is indeductible. True story: there is no free lunch. God is unabolishable. How, then, can profit—and capital, and capitalism—

be based on the *accumulation* of income *which cannot exist* in the first place? Where is capitalism getting its free lunch? Where is Livingstone *extracting* his fame as an explorer? Why has the position of equilibrium seemingly *not moved* to counteract the occultic Livingstonian extraction? How have Chuma and Susi been occultically—magically—*deducted* from the record?

We know that for there to be capitalism, capital must exist as a thing. Surplus value must be guaranteed. The problem is that this is only possible if capitalism is a *perpetual motion machine of the first kind*, which reproduces surplus value and typically produces profit after deducting cost. That is, its profits have *no* costs in them. But this is absurd. Capitalism is absurd because it claims to be able to *deduct* costs! Such a perpetual motion machine violates *every rule* of life and physics. Such algorithms cannot exist. Such things violate and abolish God. The basis on which perpetual motion machines of the first kind cannot exist is the same basis on which capitalism is impossible. What *algorithm* is this, I ask, that can deduct costs? How *does* it deduct costs?

The truth is that capitalism does not really deduct costs. Rather, it merely *transforms* them into *something else*. The truth is that capital does not and cannot exist. This truth is immutable, cannot change, and capitalism knows it, too. Whatever Karl Marx saw being reproduced from the labor of workers in Volume 1 of *Capital* could not have been capital. Capital cannot be produced, because it cannot exist; capital does not exist, and therefore cannot be produced. This *spectrality* of capital is fundamental to the whole thesis of apartheid. If costs are like energy which can neither be created nor destroyed but can only be *transformed* from one form to another, it becomes clear that capital does not really exist, but is merely the *transformation of costs* from one mode to another. Capitalism thus exists as an algorithm for abolishing God, and, crucially, *for keeping God abolished*. That is, capitalism is a gigantic hoax: it is a mechanism for making it seem *as if* profits can exist. Capitalism exists *as if* capital can exist, and capital itself exists *as if* it were *costless*. We are faced with a sort of spectrum, at the one end of which is *costlessness*, and at the other is this constant *as-if-ness*. This *as-if-ness* is capitalism's greatest triumph. That is, *the triumph of capitalism is capitalism* itself. Capitalism's singular *coup* is that it exists at all. Indeed, its highest material achievement to date remains *that* singular act of abolishing God.

If we have established that capital, profit, and capitalism are elements of a perpetual machine of the first kind, what is next? We have said that they *do not* and *cannot* exist. But, surely, this is only half the story. We are still to reach the latter steps of the algorithm, before it *stops* and repeats its perpetual action. We still need to understand how capitalism abolishes God. Is God at all abolishable? Is it not the height of hubris to even try to violate and abolish God? That is, *how can one have a free lunch*? We know this to be impossible. How can one make something out of nothing? How can a thing—in this case, capital—*not* have a price? How has the impossible become possible and the possible become impossible? The answer is both plain and circular. Capitalism abolishes God through its greatest single innovation: *cost cutting*. Ultimately, capitalist modernity and the wealth of nations are nothing more than the *cutting of cost*. The answer edges us closer to understanding the true identity of the wealth of nations.

Still, the algorithm has some more steps to run before hitting STOP because we need to establish definitively what we really mean and do not mean by *cost cutting*. This is important because *we know that costs cannot actually be cut*.[21] Only a perpetual machine of the first kind can cut costs, and we know that such a machine cannot exist. So, what do people really mean when they talk about cutting costs? Some speak about slashing costs, others about reducing them, keeping them low, tightening belts, living within our means, and so on. How does one do this? How does one *tighten* a belt?

The circular *as-if-ness* of capital says that to cut cost out of human action, modernity needs to keep God abolished. We know that the *return of God* would immediately entail the abolition of capitalism. As we saw earlier, the two cannot coexist. There cannot be God and capitalism at the same time, for capital is what pretends to *replace* God. That is, capital is the new God, the *replacement* maintained by the illusion that surplus value and profits are real.

This circularity establishes a paradox: the rule that capitalism *has* to *violate* in order to exist is the first and most important rule it needs to *observe* in order to survive at all. In order to be, it must cease to be. What really is going on?

To understand this apparent paradox, we must begin at the beginning. The greatest wish of any capitalist is that things did not come with a cost. Capitalists wish *they did not have to pay* anything at all for the profits they make. Their singular *obsession with cost* is precisely so that they could abolish it—forever. That is, we all know that capitalists need to cut costs in order to realize profits. There is universal agreement about this. But how can expensive things *be without expense*? This seems to be a kind of magic, a kind of alchemy. As we just noted, profits are made to *seem real* by cutting costs. That is, profits are possible *only if* expenses are subtracted and deducted. This subtraction is itself only possible if the principle of *the natural cost of everything* is violated. The algorithm for cutting cost out of human action is, of course, what I call *apartheid*. But more of that later. For now, we need to establish the *nature* and *maintenance* of the wealth of nations. It is important to see that the nature of the wealth of nations actually lies in the principle of cost, in the natural price of things. Such wealth is neither created nor destroyed but is merely *transformed*. That is, Adam Smith is wrong to talk of the *causes* of the wealth of nations. The proper term is *transformation*. There is no cause and effect here. Nothing, as far as we know, is being caused. Nothing is really happening. We are, in fact, really in the realm of magic. Magic, as we know, is the opposite of reality, the opposite of God.

So how does capitalism *transform* wealth? What sort of magic is this? In answering this question, we would

---

[21] Such that to say that one *cuts costs* is only a manner of speaking. The phrase is thus to be understood either as a figure of speech or should be enclosed in quotation marks.

have answered the riddle of modernity. In addressing this question, we would have understood Apartheid Studies. Indeed, this whole project of Apartheid Studies turns precisely on demonstrating just such a relation.

The answer is as follows. Since we have demonstrated that *cost* can never *truly* go away, capitalist modernity has to come up with an insurance scheme. This scheme is a simple step in the algorithm: *to make others live with the cost*. That is, capitalists *make others pay the price*. Someone else *bears* the burden. This is the only fool proof way to make costs "disappear." The perpetual motion machine of the first kind does not actually run forever. It does not actually run on no energy. It is not really and truly costless. Rather, *someone else*, somewhere, bears the interminable cost of the disappearance of God. The Eternity of Cost is merely *invoiced, billed,* and *levied* somewhere else. The name that I give to these *bodies that are made available for purposes of cost cutting* is *blackbodies*. Blackbodies are needed because *nature abhors a vacuum*. When capitalism abolished God, it raised blackbodies in God's place. This is the nature of the *replacement* that constitutes the wealth of nations.

The Shona saying *munhu munhu*[22] (a human being is a human being; a person is a person) is central to our understanding of the eternal battle between God and capital. *Munhu munhu* is the maxim that a human being remains, indivisibly, inviolably, a human being: a person is, inalienably, a person, and will always be so, whatever their livelihood. Only God can change that. That is, only God can make things *be* what He calls them ("Let there be Light," or some such command). This power—or unabolishability—of God is precisely what is meant by the power of exemption. Capital, through the algorithms and charters of apartheid, also makes claims on this power of exemption. That is, apartheid also wants people to become what it calls them—the power to make people necessarily become what they are called.

To say *munhu munhu*, therefore, is in fact not to repeat a word, but, rather, to affirm the *indivisibility, inviolability,* and *untransformability* of a human being. A human being is *untransformable*—he or she cannot be transformed into anything else other than a human being. Only objects (chattel) can be transformed into what they are not, as illustrated by the *Dred Scott v. Sandford* case (1857) in the United States Supreme Court. After all, a slave does not really exist in the first place—a slave is merely a figment, a *wish* of the slave-master's imagination.[23] What

---

[22] In the Nguni languages the phrase is "Umuntu ngumuntu" or "Motho ke motho," and it is the first, central clause in the well-known aphorism: "Umuntu ngumuntu ngabantu," translated as, "A person is a person with other persons," or "With other persons, a person is a person."

[23] Since the slave is merely an expression of the *wish* of the master, slavery also is a wish of the master. By *wish* I mean a futile attempt to conceal what is really going on. That is, slavery is *really* institutionalized theft of the work of one human being by another human being. It is in this sense that slavery can only end with the *return* of stolen wealth. Most attention on slave holdings and the plantation system has failed to devote adequate attention or argument to the fact that slaves were, in fact, essential to the very existence of the "master" and "his" plantation. That is, slaves were the actual dispossessed owners of the whole system of property and money being generated by

exists, rather, is a *human being* whom the master *regards* as a slave. But, as the notion of *munhu munhu* shows, a human being remains, indivisibly, a human being. The wish of the slave-master is not a Godly command like, "Let there be Light." Just because you wish me to be a slave does not make me *into* a slave. Indeed, I cannot be made into a slave even if I want, wish, need, require, and desire to be a slave. This is the sense in which to say *munhu munhu* is not repetition or saying a word twice. Rather, *munhu munhu* means that human being is a human being *first* before being *called* a human being. Even a poor person, a thug, or a criminal is a human being.

Munhu munhu means that a human being is a human being, even if he or she were not *called* a human being. A human being is a human being because he or she is a human being, not because he or she is called a human being. As the philosopher Archie Mafeje suggests, things are not necessarily what they are called (253).[24]

One rather simple way of understanding the abolition of *munhu* and the question of the wealth of nations is to reconsider the phenomenon of slavery in the United States, West Indies, South Africa, and so on, between the 1500s and the 1800s, up to the point of its abolition. In 1833, Britain supposedly abolished slavery throughout the British Empire with the passage of the Slavery Abolition Act. French colonies re-abolished it in 1848. The United States did so in 1865 via the 13th Amendment. But all this abolishing is *in reality* fake news. Slavery will always be with us as long as capitalism is with us. This is because the question of slavery is fairly and squarely a question of the wealth of nations, a question of profit. How so? The big question that faced promoters and practitioners of slavery, from the big banks to governments, insurers, plantation owners, and slave masters was how to find the *perfect slave*: one that did not lose value. How is a *perfect slave* produced? We have already demonstrated that this sort of *perfectibility*—or deductibility—is as impossible as a perpetual machine of the first kind. Interestingly, it is the quest for the *perfect slave* that defines capitalism, capitalist modernity, and modernity.

Again, in order to understand the reproduction of the *perfect slave*, we need to begin at the beginning. Before the abolition of slavery, the slave functioned as an inefficient *store of value*. That is, the slave was *compelled to be available* whenever the slave-master needed him or her, whether for labor, to be raped, traded, auctioned, or *exchanged*. However, this system was *inefficient* because the slave-master had to *cause* the slave to be available. The act of *causing the availability* of slaves is always already costly, since it requires the perpetual presence of the slave-master and the slave-driver. That is the *opportunity cost* is undeniable. A slave is perpetually losing value because he or she is a living, breathing, sentient human being. The purpose of abolition in 1833 was thus precisely to *transform* this inefficient, costly practice of storing value *in* slaves. That is, no slave was ever willingly and voluntarily

---

their blood, muscle, skin, bone and sweat. The master was a mere impostor.

[24] Mafeje, Archie. "The Ideology of 'Tribalism.'" *The Journal of Modern African Studies*, vol. 9, no. 2, pp. 253-261.

available to be a slave. He or she *had to be made into* a slave. Essentially, the slave was an *illiquid* store of value. The opportunity cost of driving slaves ultimately made slavery inefficient and thus sealed its fate. Indeed, it is these *inevitable costs* of slavery that fundamentally explain its abolition. Had slavery been *costless*, it would *never* have ended. As such, a new way of storing value had to be evolved. The answer was to "free" the slaves.

But what does it *really* mean to free the slaves? The freeing of slaves is a *transformation*. We spoke above of the operation of magic, of a mode of *as-if-ness*. To free the slaves thus means abolishing not slavery itself, but the opportunity cost of driving slaves. How does one abolish the opportunity cost of driving slaves? The answer lies in freeing slaves *to drive themselves*. We spoke above of the singular innovation of capitalism in terms of the magic of *transformation* and the abolition of God, where a thing is able to *be where it is not* and *not be where it is*. Something has happened, yet it has not. Something has not happened, yet it has: a kind of Schrödinger's cat. The "freeing" of slaves is a *transformation* in this sense. Slaves are never really freed.[25] They merely undergo a *transformation*. Slavery itself never really ends.[26] It is merely *transformed*.

To understand the "freeing" of slave as *transformation*, one needs to think, analogically, of the so-called free-range chickens. Although such chickens range freely, they are *still* chickens. Despite ranging freely, free-range chickens are still chickens. That is, they range freely without any loss of *chickenness*. They are *perfect* chickens. Despite a *transformation* in their condition, they retain their original function. That is, they roam *freely* outdoors in the sunlight and have extensive locomotion, but at the end of the day, they are still *available to be eaten* just like their confined counterparts. *There is no loss of value.* Indeed, some chicken eaters imagine that free range chickens taste *even better* than cooped up chickens. Hence, the abolition of slavery is the *ultimate cost saving* measure because it creates the *perfect slave*.

The *perfect slave* is the slave who drives himself or herself without needing a slave-driver, one who is *perpetually available* without being caused to be so. This perfect slave is the blackbody, the *currency of modernity*. Slavery is abolished precisely in order to *transform* the slave *into* perfection: the blackbody. Slavery is thus abolished by being made ineffable. In this case, the *transformation* functions mainly to conceal. The blackbody is thus a free-range slave, the *perfect slave* who retains purchasing power into the future. Prior to abolition, the costly physical presence of a slave-driver was essential in order to ensure the perpetual

---

[25] This is because, as we have shown, a slave does not really exist in the first place—a slave is merely a figment, a *wish* (see the next footnote for an articulation of "wish") of the slave-master's imagination. What exists, rather, is a *human being* whom the master *regards* as a slave.

[26] As noted earlier, slavery is a wish of the master in the same sense that the slave is merely an expression of the *wish* of the master. *Wish* here articulates a futile attempt to conceal what is really going on: that slavery is *really* the institutionalized theft of the work of one human being by another human being and can only end with the *return* of stolen wealth—a return that marks the disappearance of America and Europe as we know them. Since Europe and America have not disappeared, slavery has not ended.

availability of the slave. The slave of the sugar cane fields of the West Indies, the plantations of Virginia, and the wine farms of South Africa's Western Cape could not be perpetually adjusted for inflation. After abolition, however, the physical presence of the slave-master is no longer necessary, thus taking the cost *out* of slavery. Essentially, abolition is *in truth* the abolition of the cost of slavery. That is, abolition is a form of risk management and risk absorption: the slave becomes *even more valuable* because of abolition. A slave who is not called a slave is infinitely more valuable than a slave called a slave. To advocate abolishing slavery, but without abolishing capitalism, is to be an agent of lies for we know that there is no freedom under capitalism. Under capitalism there are only *transformations*. The freed slave becomes a new, free-range being: the blackbody. The blackbody, as we will continuously discover, is the true wealth of nations. This is because the freed or free-range slave has a newly found *liquidity*. He or she is a perpetual store of value, always adjustable for inflation and always available to resolve budget deficits. The disappearance, or the newly found ineffability of the slave-master and the slave-driver has meant a "disappearance" of the opportunity costs of slavery. But where have the costs disappeared *to*? The costs have not really disappeared. The costs, as we saw above, do not really disappear. There is still no free lunch. There will never be a free lunch. What has changed is the presence of this new, free-range being—the blackbody. It simply means that the "freed" slave *makes himself or herself available* whether for labor, to be raped, traded, auctioned, or exchanged. This is the true definition of the *free* market. The "freedom" of the market is a function of *availability*.

This is how capitalism *transforms* wealth: it brings God back through the back door in a terminally degraded form. It finds the *perfect slave*: the *free-range being*. The story of this degraded God of-the-backdoor, of the slums and of the backyards, who mostly lives in proximity of the *poverty line* in townships, shacks, barrios, compounds, favelas, hostels, dungles, and rubbish dumps, who dies, is diseased and violated *in large numbers*, is the real subject of Apartheid Studies. This, then, is how blackbodies turn out to be the insurance scheme of modernity: capital abolishes God in order to resurrect him in a *new form*. This is how the wealth of nations is transformed and maintained: through keeping *in the world* a ready and valuable *store* of blackbodies. This, again, is a fact easily established: blackbodies are God.

Basically, the only time that we find capitalists acknowledging God is *when someone else is paying the price* and *footing the bill*. In Conrad's *Heart of Darkness*, Marlow describes a train of European ivory traders perched on donkeys arriving at a trading station:

> [E]ach section [was] headed by a donkey carrying a white man in new clothes and tan shoes, bowing from that elevation right and left to the impressed pilgrims. A quarrelsome band of *footsore* sulky niggers trod on the heels of the donkey; a lot of tents, camp-stools, tin boxes, white cases, brown bales would be shot down in the courtyard (66,

emphasis added) (1987: 66).

Once again, the Livingstone paradox is in full demonstration here: the white men ride on donkeys in new clothes and tan shoes, and it is left to the black men to be *footsore*. The blackbody is *footsore* on account it does the *footing*, carrying tents, camp-stools, tin boxes, cases, bales, and whatnot. The blackbody is thus *footsore* because it actually has to use its *feet*. Essentially, it is the blackbody's *feet* which directly *exempt* the white traders from doing any carrying. The *elevation* of the white traders is a function of the pitter-patter of the blackbody's *feet*. The *footing of the bill* thus emerges as an element of the charters and algorithms of apartheid. As Marlow says, "Strings of dusty niggers *with splay feet* arrived and departed; a stream of manufactured goods, rubbishy cottons, beads, and brass-wire set into the depths of darkness, and in return came a precious trickle of ivory" (51, emphasis added). As the splay feet arrive and depart, so are the profits made.

This, then, ought to be the proper definition of capitalism: *the act of making someone else foot the bill*. It is the act of making someone else *meet* the cost. This is also the crucial, yet simple, principle behind modernity and globalization. Capitalism is an attempt to *make someone else carry the cost* of doing business—to cost, levy, bill, and invoice someone else. Hence: "Expensive" minus "Expense" = Capitalism.

As stated, the entities that are reproduced and made available to foot the bill are none other than blackbodies. The process of making blackbodies *available* is apartheid. Simply put, capitalism is an attempt to make the action of capital *to not have to pay its own costs*. Rather, God must foot the bill.

How does one ascertain the *cost of capital*? I believe that we will never be able to properly define the wealth of nations *until* we arrive at a true definition of the cost of capital. Currently, only economists are left to define it, but they have never been able to do a good job of it since they are only able to *model* the cost of capital in mere theoretical and abstract terms. For instance, they would have us believe, through math and spreadsheets, that the cost of capital is the rate of return that persuades any given investor to invest. Fine. But what is the real nature of this *rate*? Why do investors invest *at all*? How are things really *financed*? Who pays? What is the nature of this cost? How does one guarantee, or at least judge, whether any given cash flow will *actually* materialize? How do we deal with things about which we are quite certain? There have not been any original answers *outside* of the textbooks, the equations, and the models. I eschew abstract notions of the *cost of equity* in favor of a properly forensic study of how costs were saved when young Michael Komape died in a pit toilet at a Limpopo school, when the Grenfell Tower in London was consumed in a holocaust, when the sweatshop in Rana, Bangladesh, collapsed killing hundreds, or when in a township of Soweto a South African bank sold Solomon Nhlapo's house for a penny behind his back making him a trespasser in his own home. To my mind, this is the only way to truly judge whether any given cash flow will actually *materialize*. This is a qualitative exercise that requires that one look at *the way in which costs are cut* as opposed to thinking about opportunity cost in isolation from the worlds in which people live and die.

Komape, Grenfell Tower, Rana, and Nhlapo are valuable to the exercise of Apartheid Studies because they interfere with and disrupt the normative understandings of the *cost of capital*, the *cost of debt*, and *the cost of equity*. Indeed, Komape, Grenfell Tower, Rana, and Nhlapo, among others, are the only true means of telling whether the present value of a cash flow will stay *constant forever*. At any rate, Apartheid Studies turns on the view that the question of the *cost of capital* is too important to the future of the world and to the future of our children and grandchildren to be left to the economists. I believe that we must pose this question at a more fundamental level: the circuits, algorithms, and worlds in which blackbodies live. If and when we pose the question of capital by deferring to the evidence drawn from the mass of the everyday lives of ordinary people, we will find that the *cost of capital* is not an economic question at all but, rather, a question of *apartheid*, of power, of God, of modernity, and of the wealth of nations. It is a fundamentally *deeper* question that requires integrated fields of study that reconsider the meanings of the circuits, algorithms, and worlds in which we live. This is what I have called Apartheid Studies: the study of the nature and maintenance of the wealth of nations. *Apartheid Studies* contemplates the fullness of the lives of blackbodies.

BY WAY OF CONCLUSION

Apartheid Studies is the study of *password exemptions* that structure and underlie modernity from South Africa to Brazil, Palestine to Bangladesh, Bulgaria to the United Kingdom, Angola to Australia, Kenya to Canada, United States to Uganda. Password exemption is the fundamental relation on which modernity is built. That relation is what I identify as *apartheid*. My thesis is that blackbodies are the true *wealth of nations*. Without them, there is no modernity. Without blackbodies, there is *nothing*. To demonstrate the nature of the blackbody and its centrality to global capitalist modernity, we can draw on the example of the parasitic fungus, *O. unilateralis s.l.*

O. unilateralis s.l is a body-thieving fungus that parasitizes and zombifies the bodies of the carpenter ant host *Camponotus castaneus* in the rain forests of Brazil. The *modus operandi* of this puppeteer fungus is to control the actions and movements of the zombified host, altering and manipulating its reflexes in ways that cause it to abandon its tree top habitat and migrate to the forest floor where the fungus needs to be in order to reproduce suitably. The parasite takes over the body, muscles, fibers, tissue, and reflexes of the ant. Researchers have been puzzled by the fact that the fungus appears to be interested in taking over the body only: it leaves the brain intact. As Fredericksen and her colleagues point out, "behavior control does not require the parasite to physically invade the host brain" 12590).[27] Rather, fungal pathogens infiltrate ant muscle tissue. It is the

---

[27] Fredericksen, Maridel A., et al. "Three-Dimensional Visualization and a Deep-Learning Model Reveal Complex Fungal Parasite Networks in Behaviorally Manipulated

body, it seems, that has always been at issue. Indeed, biologists have found that fungus *O. unilateralis s.l.* is "present throughout the Body" (Fredericksen 12591). This fungus literally drives and steers the conscious but hapless ant to the underside of a leaf, where the ant anchors itself with its powerful mandibles until it dies. Meanwhile, the fungus inside the *dead-alive* ant never stops growing and festering. Eventually it punctures its way out of the ant's body via the head, releasing fungal spores which reproduce and trap yet more ants. Just like *O. unilateralis* proliferates throughout the entire host's body, from head to thorax, abdomen to legs, so does apartheid *possess* the blackbody. The distribution, abundance, and interactions of the fungus inside the body of its manipulated host is nearly total. It is a *systemic takeover*.

The apartheid fungus infects, infiltrates and takes over its host in such a way that the ant is no longer an ant; it is really fungus in ant's guise. That is, the host is an externalised version of the apartheid fungus. Zombified ants look like ants from the outside but in reality they are no longer 100% ants, for they have become part insect, part fungus, a process known as *extended phenotype*. Extended phenotype means that *O. unilateralis* has snatched another being's body and turned that hijacked body into a literal extension of its own physical self. The fungus causes changes in host gene expression, perhaps chemically altering its brain for its own purposes. Fredericksen et al. find that:

[T]he *altered host behavior* is an *extended phenotype* of a microbial parasite's genes being *expressed through the body* of an animal. An important question to ask is how these microbes, which are much smaller than their hosts, can control animal behavior to produce such *spectacular extended phenotypes*. (12590, emphasis added)

The notion of *extended phenotype* is critical to the study of apartheid. For instance, it allows us to see how an arch-imperialist such as Rhodes *extends his phenotype* into Africa and Africans by way of the "Native Bill of Africa," the Glen Grey Act. The *extension of phenotype* explains colonialism, empire, slavery, capitalism, and most other forms of violent, systemic parasitism that are at the heart of modernity. We would have done half our job in Apartheid Studies if we were able to read *Rhodes as fungus* (his true actions in reality are that of a body-snatching fungus, more insidious and long-lasting than visible and short-term), *capitalism as fungus* (its true action in reality operates at deeper, body-snatching spectral levels), and blackbodies as fungus-filled, fungible bodies (they are dead-alive, controlled peripherally, through the world's stock exchanges).

O. unilateralis steers and navigates the ant, or what is left of it, towards the forest floor and towards the leaf where it is to die. The ant's brain can see and sense what is going on but cannot do anything about it because its body no longer belongs to it. Its body is no longer its own. Instead, it has become a blackbody. It is in this sense that a

---

Ants." *PNAS*, vol. 114, no. 47, pp. 12590-95.

blackbody is a captured, infiltrated, hijacked body. It is a body that can be induced to do anything that the fungus orders and desires. Hence:

> Fungal cells were found throughout the host body but not in the brain, implying that behavioral control of the animal body by this microbe occurs peripherally. Additionally, fungal cells invaded host muscle fibers and joined together to form networks that encircled the muscles. These networks may represent a collective foraging behavior of this parasite, which may in turn facilitate host manipulation. (Fredericksen 12590)

This kind of apartheid parasitism of the body directly contradicts the Cartesian cogito. Can the parasitized ant, with its whole body infiltrated and captured, still be called an ant? Is it still an ant or is now a fungus? One of the researchers who discovered that the fungus leaves the brain intact says, "We found that a high percentage of the cells in a host were fungal cells. In essence, these manipulated animals were a fungus in ants' clothing."[28]

The reality of the blackbody presents a specific refutation of the vaunted Cartesian cogito, for it shows that whoever controls the body controls the being and its world. One can go on *thinking* but ceases to exist to all intents and purposes. *I think, but still I am not*. All the apartheid fungus needs to do is abolish the ant as a living being. Bioactive compounds, as neuromodulators, go to work on the body of the host and the host's legs and mandibles become the fungus' own legs and mandibles. What is crucial is not to manipulate and control the mind at all, but, rather, to control and manipulate the circadian clock and the circadian rhythms of human beings. Essentially, the apartheid fungus' spectacular innovation is to *externalize* the biological clock out of the ant and appropriate it for itself. What are we without our bodies? The whole Apartheid Studies paradigm thus turns on this fact: the theft and externalization of the body. Once one loses the biological clock to the factory floor, the mine shaft, the shift, capitalism, or a slave driver, one enters directly or indirectly into the inhuman rhythms of apartheid. It is thus the parasitic control of our biological clocks, by things outside of ourselves, which turns us into blackbodies. An example would be the lives of the laborers of Johannesburg gold mines, whose circadian rhythms have been externalized into the shifts of the mine shaft, the residential compound, and the contract. The study of apartheid is thus the study of parasite-host interactions: the daily rhythms and circadian clocks into which we are plugged. Human beings not in ownership of the rhythms of their bodies cease to exist. They think even though they are not. They are available to modernity not as human beings but as blackbodies—as instruments of shock absorption.

Due to *password exemption*, it is no longer certain that the bad things done to blackbodies are necessarily bad.

---

[28] Dvorsky, George. "The Fungus That Turns Ants into Zombies Is More Diabolical Than We Realized." *Gizmodo,* 11 September 2018, gizmodo.com/the-fungus-that-turns-ants-into-zombies-is-more-diaboli-1820301538. Accessed 5 March 2019.

That is, the blackbody is alchemical and *transformative*. Hence, when Cyril Ramaphosa, a billionaire businessman and the deputy president of South Africa, wrote an email describing the miners striking against the Lonmin Corporation as "dastardly criminals," the email coincided with the fact that at least 34 miners were massacred by the police a few days later. A commissioned enquiry absolved Ramaphosa of all blame. Ramaphosa himself went on record to say that his conscience told him that he had, in fact, saved more lives. It might seem ironic that Ramaphosa—a shareholder, the owner of 9% of Lonmin, and a non-executive director on the Lonmin board at the time of the massacre—made his billions from "black empowerment." But if one thinks of the massacre of blackbodies from the perspective of Apartheid Studies, the irony and contradiction vanishes. The blackbody is *transformative*. It absolves crimes and disappears crime scenes. To kill blackbodies is not necessarily the same as killing human beings. It is, rather, a bit like shooting at diseased dogs: one kills them for their own good. That is, one is doing them a favor. Ramaphosa is thus not to blame for the massacre of dastardly criminals. Indeed, he is to be praised. He did what had to be done: sacrifice approximately 34 blackbodies to save lives. We thus must *thank* Ramaphosa not for murder, but for saving lives. After all, his conscience tells him he saved lives. For this reason, he sleeps well at night. In the end, Ramaphosa never murdered anyone. At least, that is what the Marikana Commission of Inquiry appeared to prove.

The *supply*, *maintenance* and *allocation* of fungible blackbodies—what Donald Trump would categorize as the shitholes of the world—is the true task of apartheid. To my mind, nothing quite explains world history as the presence or absence of an *ideal piece of material*, surface, or cavity *that refuses nothing* but, rather, responds to change and transformation *perfectly* through absorbing and accepting *all* manner of crises, blows, harms, pain, falsehoods, lies, distortions, scars, harshness, trauma, evictions, starvations, stress positions, minimum wages, decelerations and accelerations falling on it without *exception*. The *spectrum* of the black body is meant *to absorb*; it must not complain. As a piece of *sacrificial matter*, it is not meant to choose or prefer what happens to it.

Ultimately, the plausibility of the narrative of blackbodies and Apartheid Studies appears to hinge on specific interpretations of the viability of the worlds and times in which we live. It is in this sense that *everything comes back to blackbodies*, but not in the way that we commonly suppose. The concept of blackbodies is overlooked in considering the question of the wealth of nations because we rarely look at the world through the inventories, lenses, stories, and narratives of *those who bear its costs*. Everything changes the moment we experience it through the scars and burdens of those who bear the costs of modernity. In the real world, blackbodies are those beings that are *always available* to *foot* and *meet* the inevitable cost. When we talk about a *minimum wage*, it is them we are talking about, since we cannot live on a minimum wage ourselves. When we talk about tightening belts, it is their belts we have in mind. As such, blackbodies are marked by the *certainty* of their *availability*. Being those instruments with which we come closest to 100% certainty, blackbodies are what we ultimately base decisions on. Hence, everything we can think of, everything that matters, is a function of blackbodies, since blackbodies are those beings that are screwed, over and over again, without end. They are, to put it another way, *the eternally screwed*. Basically, with blackbodies *in place*, there is little need to adjust the interest rate to account for risk. As I said earlier, the blackbody is the perfect slave. There is no need for spreadsheets or for toting up a formal discount rate. This is because black bodies come already *risk adjusted*. That is, with blackbodies there is *no* opportunity cost. After all, all blackbodies share the same *discount rate*. One blackbody has the same value as another blackbody regardless of whether it is from Zimbabwe, Ukraine, Brazil, Bangladesh, Singapore, Australia, Burkina Faso, Palestine, or Canada, or from the year 1492, 1652, 1910, 1948, 2020, 2072, or 2230. Blackbodies are those things that one expects to *always extract more from* and to *always earn more from*. They are the *optimal investment*--the reason future cash flows are discounted.

Thus, this is the essence of *apartheid modernity*: to be *risk free*. The *nature of* apartheid modernity is the subject of this keynote address. The question is: how does one arrive at a risk-free rate? The reason there is *no risk* is because global capitalists *invest in* blackbodies—the people whose bodies absorb *all* the costs. These absorbent bodies that are *maybe not 100%* human come closest to guaranteeing 100% certainty for investment decisions. For instance, billionaire investor Warren Buffett—the "Oracle of Omaha"—claims that one of his core investment secrets is to buy *discounted stocks*. We have seen, however, that the notion of *discount* is ultimately an illusion since someone else, in some place somewhere, bears the cost and foots the bill. In the same way that there is no free lunch, there is no risk-free investment. So, what does Buffet *actually* invest in? What is the real meaning of the words "risk-free"? The answer is that Buffet invests in blackbodies: those who bear the cost of costlessness. What is discounted in the price of stock is ultimately paid for by a child falling and dying in a pit toilet in Limpopo, South Africa, a man dying in trailer fire in Yazoo City, Mississippi, a child crying for its parents at the United States-Mexico border, or a Palestinian man with a teargas canister lodged in his face. Living in a shack in Imizamo Yethu, dying in a collapsing sweatshop in Rana, Bangladesh, or in a favela in Rocinha, Rio, is what constitutes the *true cost* of capital. That is, I can find no other objective measure of the cost of capital.

If we listen to Buffett, it appears that he prefers investing be best defined through a thing's "intrinsic value" arrived at through applying, for instance, a "margin of safety." The *more certain* the *discount*, the better and higher the margin of safety. But, stripped of the financial obfuscation, what does this *really* mean? Basically, the margin of safety is the shock absorber against modernity's crises. This is where blackbodies, who we have established to be the eternal shock absorbers, come in. The *intrinsic value* of blackbodies is that they absorb *austerity*. Their true value is that they are available to absorb all kinds of shock from tightening of belts to living on a minimum wage. We know, for instance, that every form of economic "recovery" is achieved on the backs of the desperately poor: these are the only people who can afford to tighten their belts *without end* but also without collapsing the world. Blackbodies never seem to go anywhere: they seem to always be *available* when needed and to be *held in place* to absorb modernity's *exemptions*. For instance, blackbodies are there when we imagine that minimum wage or riot police might be a solution. When South African politician Cyril Ramaphosa asked that "concomitant action" be taken against striking platinum miners, within a few days 34 of them had been shot dead by the police. They are *certain* to be *available* whenever there is a worrying difference between cash inflows and outflows and a need to cut back on certain expenditures. They are *certain* to be *available* when the housing waiting list gets longer than the number of houses that are being built, such that some will have to miss out and find *somewhere else* to live. They are *certain* to be there when you run into evidence of "unsustainable spending" and need to do something about it. Blackbodies are *certain* to be *available* when cuts to spending previously planned on education and healthcare are imagined. They are *certain* to be there when creditors put the pressure on, when budgets need to be "alleviated" and spending needs to be aggressively tackled, when we imagine a cut, or a freeze, without raises, and when we think about layoffs. They are always there. It is this *availability* which generates the *certainty*. Hence, the *more certain* the *discount*, the better and higher the margin of safety. No wonder, then, that it does seem that the big money is *in* these poor wretches. "Intrinsic value," therefore, seems to me to be the number of blows and crises that a large enough number of blackbodies can take during lifetime. To understand this, we must return to the parable illustrating the intrinsic value of the life of live bait as it sits and waits in the fisherman's livewell tank. Locked into vicious algorithms of poverty, shortages, lack, failure, and debt, repeated over and over again (with the proceeds automatically and conveniently pocketed by credit providers), blackbodies provide the world's *margin of safety*.

After all, the algorithms and circuits of apartheid that hold blackbodies *in place* seek to hold them there *forever*. "When we're looking at a business," says Buffet, "we're looking at holding it forever."[29] Simply put, blackbodies are the ultimate *security* without which investors would not invest. Blackbodies are the true cost of capital that persuades any given investor to invest. Put another way, blackbodies are an *opportunity*. They are an opportunity to rob, rape, manipulate, use, abuse, dump, enslave, abandon, exploit, extort, murder, injure, poison, mutilate, or evict without having to account for any of it. Indeed, where blackbodies are *in place*, there is no need to waste one's time doing the math. Blackbodies are the simplest perpetual annuity formula one can find, the quickest and best way of valuing the security of modernity. In

---

[29] "Warren Buffett's Discount Rate." *Warren Buffet on Investment*, 27 August 2013, warrenbuffettoninvestment.com/warren-buffetts-discount-rate/. Accessed on 7 June 2017.

simple terms, the viability of global capitalist modernity as we know it is determined by the inflows and outflows of blackbodies, discounted at an appropriate interest rate, of course. That is, the blackbody is the only common yardstick, the only standard of measurement, that satisfies the kinds of margins of safety that modernity needs to remain viable. Blackbodies thus constitute the fundamental structural moat that secures modernity. It maintains and locks in *large enough holdings* of blackbodies in the world to offset crises and absorb panics and shocks. Once secured, one no longer needs to worry too much about crises or even to watch blackbodies too closely. Indeed, with a shock absorber *in place*, there are, in fact, no panics, surprises, or crises. Here we arrive at a major thesis of Apartheid Studies: our modern times are a function of blackbodies. Without blackbodies there is nothing. In an uncertain world, blackbodies are the determining variable. That is, they are the *equity of nations*.

This analysis allows us to carefully study our modern times and how they are underwritten. How, for instance, does one determine modernity's overall health? Apartheid Studies demonstrates this by consistently assessing modernity's very own *fundamentals*. But what are those fundamentals? The short answer is, again, blackbodies. You determine the overall health of modernity by looking at *how deep* its *holdings of blackbodies* are. I will give an example. The South African gold industry was in trouble after the Anglo-Boer War (1899-1902). All of a sudden, very few blackbodies could be found to be put to work as cheap labor. To put it bluntly, *the mines had no future prospects*. Without a *guarantee* of blackbodies, the Rand Mines were at the risk of default and facing imminent liquidation. The business of the Rand Mines would have to be brought to an end and its assets distributed to claimants, creditors, and shareholders. The solution was to borrow more blackbodies by importing the Chinese. In this way, the holdings were temporarily improved.

This analysis shows that the true value of the gold mines lay in the availability of blackbodies that the Chamber of Mines assisted by the state, foreign governments, and global capital could *summon at will*. This *summoning at will* is a critical measure. Essentially, any industry or institution that cannot *summon at will* whatever it *fundamentally needs* will soon collapse. However, the only way to *summon at will* whatever one needs is to lock in and maintain large holdings and reserves of it. This maintenance of blackbodies is the task of apartheid. It was to ensure large holdings of blackbodies that Cecil Rhodes devised the "Native Bill for Africa," in the form of the Glen Grey Act of 1894. Bantustans, townships, slums, compounds, and hostels make sense only in the context of apartheid as the systematic maintenance and locking in of large numbers of living blackbodies in order to ensure the future of modernity. Modernity makes sense only in the context of such no-nonsense *leverage*. Indeed, modernity is the most leveraged institution of all propped up as it is by the large holdings of blackbodies. Basically, blackbodies are the reason modernity can never default. That is, blackbodies are how modernity is underwritten, serviced, and financed. Without them, there is nothing. Apartheid, then, is how modernity protects itself against future shocks and crises. It is a kind of futures contract.

The concept of cost—or expenditure, or God—is thus inherently built into our bodies, into every living body, in such a way that *to live is necessarily to expend*. For instance, every action of our living bodies, however insignificant that action may be, *spends* and *expends* energy. Every single body that lives *spends* and *expends*. For something, anything, to happen, something must be spent and given up. Nothing will happen from nothing. Every movement, however small, creates a vacuum, a gap, which must be filled. As they say, nature abhors a vacuum. In order to get something, something must be given up *in its place*. There is nothing *in place of* nothing. This is the Law of Life, which explains the existence of God. The idea that *living has a cost*, therefore, provides an infinitely rich avenue of inquiry into the nature of God, modernity, and apartheid—an avenue that, it would seem, has unfortunately been limited and corrupted by the facile and unimaginative economic concepts of the cost of living, spending, expenditure, capital, and price. Freed from their economic limits, the notions of spending, expenditure, price, cost of capital, and the cost of living have a deeper theoretical significance that speaks directly to the abolition of God, *states of exemption*, *passing over*, and the extortion of the power of password exemption that allows capital, the cost of capital, and the wealth of nations to emerge.

What I want to do with Apartheid Studies is embark on a *real valuation* of modernity. A substantive and fundamental analysis shows that the cheap labor of the Rand gold mines was in fact the *real value*—the intrinsic value—of the mines. Certainly, the balance sheets of the mines would have been on fire had there been no guarantees of blackbodies. As such, what the Randlords of South Africa really owned were blackbodies, *transmuted* into shares for ease of trading on the Johannesburg Stock Exchange. To understand this, we need to get beyond the technical jargon about stocks, stock markets, stock exchanges, and exchange rates. The truth is that all this jargon conceals the operation of the algorithms of apartheid—the transmutation of blackbodies into fungible, tradable stock. Apartheid basically manages the exchange rate of blackbodies. By holding large numbers of them *in stock* in slums, favelas, barrios, townships, poor rural areas, hostels, compounds, prisons and other dark places, these blackbodies can be exchanged. The key is to lock-in all these people in the treacherous vicinity of the *breadline*. Without a guaranteed store of blackbodies, the Johannesburg gold mines could not go onto the stock exchange since they had not stock to exchange. Hence the true stock are blackbodies. The *real* and *substantive value* of the gold mines were blackbodies.

It is a truism that the stock market is perhaps the most vital component of a free-market economy. Its purpose is to provide companies with access to capital *in exchange* for giving investors a slice of ownership. But this is hardly the whole story. What really is the true nature of the stock market? What is the stock that is being exchanged? The fundamental question that is not asked is what *investors* are being invited to own. If we go back to our example of the Witwatersrand gold mines following the Anglo-Boer War, it is clear that no investors would have invested in the mines at the end of the war had there been no plan and no guarantee that blackbodies would sooner or later be *somehow found and retained for as long as possible* to cheaply work the mines. Therefore, we know that investors at a stock exchange are *in fact* invited to own the holdings of blackbodies that companies have or claim to have now and in the future. I thus propose that the only true way to assess the future of modernity is to look at its holdings of blackbodies. Blackbodies are a market's true value, and the depth of holdings of blackbodies is the only true formula for figuring out *intrinsic value*. I aver that when we talk of stock holding, a fundamental analysis will always lead us to blackbodies. It is blackbodies that are exchanged on the stock market. It is blackbodies that are the stock, just as plantation slaves on the auction block were stock

We are our mobile screen ... "We wear all mankind as our skin":[1] The Mobile Phone and the Structure of Experience

ALBERTO JOSÉ LUIS CARRILLO CANÁN

BENEMÉRITA UNIVERSIDAD AUTÓNOMA DE PUEBLA
PUEBLA, MEXICO

ABSTRACT: *This text hast three parts: the first is concerned with the concept of form or structure of experience, the second part is devoted to the "electric form" of the experience, and the third part discusses the electric form of the experience generated by the mobile phone. Finally, the text explores the form of the political fostered by the mobile phone as smart phone.*

KEYWORDS: structure of experience, attitude of mind, mobile phone, smart phone, compressionality, compassionality, electric form.

This text has three parts: the first is concerned with the concept of form or structure of experience, the second part is devoted to what McLuhan calls "electric form" of the experience, and the third part discusses the electric form of the experience generated by the mobile phone. Finally, the text explores the form of the political fostered by the mobile phone as a smartphone.

1. THE MEDIATIC STRUCTURE OR FORM OF THE EXPERIENCE

Marshall McLuhan advanced the concept of the "form of experience" as related to technologies or to specific media (*Understanding Media* 78, 190).[1] His idea is that the use of any media generates a cognitive pattern or cognitive mental set correlated with a behavioral pattern.[2] More broadly, for McLuhan media environments correlate with definite mental sets or attitudes, which leads him to his well-known theory of the oral, the mechanic, and the electric ages, each dominated by a technological form—correspondingly speech, alphabet and print, and electric media—and each correlated to a well-defined mental set or "attitude of mind" (*Gutenberg Galaxy*

[†] In his introduction to the MIT Press edition of Marshall McLuhan's *Understanding Media,* Lewis H. Lapham cites some of McLuhan's more prophetic aphorisms, one of which he gives in a modified form as: "'We are the television screen ...We wear all mankind as our skin." I take further liberties with the phrase by substituting mobile phone for television screen in my title and later in the paper.

[1] In this guise McLuhan speaks, for instance, of "[m]ovies as a nonverbal form of experience ... like photography" (*Understanding Media* 285).

[2] McLuhan insists that "behavioural constraints must include constraint of thought" (*Gutenberg Galaxy* 20).

141).

It must be stressed that McLuhan really does think of structures or forms of experience. He is a formal thinker even if this is not evident from the episodic way in which he writes. Nevertheless, McLuhan's formalism asserts itself in *Understanding Media* when he refers to the "do-it-yourself *form of experience*" (168) or to the "participational or do-it-yourself *aspect* of electric technology" (158), and also to "the 'do-it-yourself' *pattern* of living" (232), where "pattern" is another term McLuhan uses for form.³ McLuhan's formal way of thinking is especially evident when he speaks of the "do-it-yourself-*ness*" (319).⁴ To the terms "form," "aspect," and "pattern," one has to add a further one, for McLuhan also speaks of the "do-it-yourself *character*" (165) and, more precisely, of the "do-it-yourself *character* that *pervades* a wide variety of *media experiences* today" (165). The last quotation is important since it explicitly considers "character"—hence "form," "aspect," and "pattern" as well—as something *present*, or using Kantian terminology from the *Critique of Pure Reason*, as a *constituent* of "a wide variety of media experiences" (*Understanding Media* 187). McLuhan is not concerned with experiences as singular entities, but with the "form" constituting or pervading "media experiences."⁵

We mentioned Kant in the former paragraph intentionally. It is possible to rethink McLuhan's formalism in Kantian terms, that is in transcendental terms. We only need to follow Kant in saying that the form of the experience, that is, the form of the phenomena, is a *constituent* of the experience, that is, of the phenomena themselves; the form makes them possible as that what they are. This is what McLuhan has in mind when he claims that the "form" or "character" or "pattern" of the experience "pervades a wide variety of … experiences": such a form makes them *possible* (*Understanding Media* 165). Analogously to Kant, McLuhan finds that the "form of experience" is the condition of possibility for having experiences in the concrete, i.e., of the phenomena. In other words, McLuhan's "form of experience" is a *transcendental* that makes experience possible. It is the *a priori* of our experiences. More precisely, it is the *a priori* of some class of them, since the use of each medium correlates with some "form of experience" or, in fact, with several of them.⁶ In *Understanding Media*, McLuhan speaks also of the "structural qualities" of each medium or class of media, so we can interchangeably utilize the terms "structure," "form," "aspect," "pattern," and "character" (165). One is entitled to use the expressions "structure" or "pattern" or "form of experience" as equivalents;

---

³ Unless otherwise indicated, emphasis in quotations is always mine.
⁴ Exactly as the formalist Heidegger would do.
⁵ I will refer to the "do-it-your-self character of experience" in the discussion that follows, but my only interest in it is to show that McLuhan bases his theory on strong formalizations, even if the episodic character of his book and the abundant references to particular situations concerning media easily conceal the formal character of McLuhan's thought.
⁶ For a comprehensive discussion of this, see "McLuhan and the Structures of the Experience. The Case of the Alphabet and the Euclidean Space," especially the section "Media and Subjectivity."

furthermore, such notions are equivalent to the contemporary "mental sets" or "cognitive patterns" correlating with specific media or media environments. It is also possible to use the terms "attitudes" or "mental postures" for transcendental forms of the experience.[7]

The mediatically conditioned mental sets pattern experiences, i.e., the phenomena as concrete events or things so far as we are conscious of them in perceiving, behaving, or thinking. Yet, such sets remain, as McLuhan says, "subliminal;" people are not conscious of them (*Understanding Media* 191). Thus, the gist of McLuhan's theory is: (a) that every medium generates a pattern or structure of experience, which he formalizes by saying that "the medium is the message" because it shapes the human relationships and the consciousness we have of them, and (b) that we are not aware of that shaping and focus rather on the "content," that is, on the envisioned use of the medium.[8]

The point of the thesis that "the medium is the message" is that in using any medium or technology we become shaped by it in the very precise sense that the medium generates a particular, definite form or structure of the experience and that we are not aware of that since we automatically pay attention to the use of the medium. We could also say that we focus on what we do with the media but are blind to what the media do to us and make of us when they generate our cognitive patterns.

Thus, media create particular mental sets of which we are not aware. Such mental sets amount to quasi-transcendentals, since they are the conditions of possibility of the phenomena, that is, of our experiences as they are in a given mediatic environment. The qualification *quasi* stresses the fact that—unlike the Kantian transcendentals—the mediatically conditioned forms of experience are not transhistorical but have the same historical character as the media conditioning them. The history of the mind correlates with the mediatic history.

2. THE "ELECTRIC FORM" OF THE EXPERIENCE

McLuhan devotes a great deal of effort to the electric technologies as creating the "electric forms" of the experience. In general, he refers to the "electric form," which correlates with the "electric media" (*Understanding Media* 105, 247). Such a form has several characters, one of them is the already mentioned "do-it-yourself character," or "do-it-yourself form of the experience," and in formal terms, via nominalization, McLuhan arrives at the "do-it-yourself-*ness*." Yet here, we will examine only two such "electric forms," compressionality and

---

[7] McLuhan himself speaks, for instance, of the "archetypes or postures of individual minds" or of the "archetypes or postures of collective consciousness" (*Gutenberg Galaxy* 267).

[8] McLuhan develops this argument thus: "'the medium is the message' because it is the medium that shapes and controls the scale and form of human association and action. The content or uses of such media are as diverse as they are ineffectual in shaping the form of human association. Indeed, it is only too typical that the 'content' of any medium blinds us to the *character* of the medium [the medium as form]" (*Understanding Media* 8).

compassionality. In *Understanding Media*, McLuhan speaks of the "compressional *character* of the electric technology" (111). Our term "compressional-*ity*" is a formalization of "compressional" via nominalization, just like McLuhan's "compressional *character*." Since McLuhan uses the expression "compassional and compressional" (84), we are likewise entitled to nominalize "compassional" to render the formal term "compassionality." Again, we must insist that, contrary to all appearances, McLuhan is a formal thinker. In fact, the hyphenation "do-it-yourself" marks a formal concept that is notoriously escalated in the nominalization "do-it-your-self-*ness*," an extremely formal expression, to dispel any doubts that McLuhan is a formalist.⁹

Compressionality amounts to the annihilation of space and time because of the speed of light making electrically mediated things and events accessible independently of (a) distance to them and of (b) elapsed time to their occurrence. McLuhan formulates the idea in many ways, for instance:

…our world has become *compressional* by dramatic reversal. As electrically contracted, the globe is no more than a village. Electric speed in bringing all social and political functions together in a sudden implosion has heightened human awareness of responsibility to an intense degree. (*Understanding Media* 5)

As far as electrically mediated experiences are (a) delocalized and (b) permanently recall-able, they acquire a mythical character. This means that having a particular experience does not depend on distance; much to the contrary, things happen as if in front of us. Since they are presented to everybody by the electric media in real time—like the attack on the Twin Towers in 2001—everybody can behold the event and experience it independently of the distance from its real occurrence. Furthermore, the event is always repeatable since it is recorded and on the web. Witnessing an event becomes like speaking to the gods: one can do it not only wherever one is but also whenever one wants to do it. That is the pure annihilation of space and time or *compression* as a form or common pattern "pervading" any electrically mediated experience, that is, a thing or event. Another paramount instance of compression is Trump's conversation about women in a dressing room. It was an event in a private space and occurred some years ago, but as soon as it was on the web and everybody got access to the event, it became delocalized and is now permanently recall-able. The recallable character of any recorded event leads Vilém Flusser to say that "technical images"—versions of McLuhan's electrically mediated events—amount to a dam of history because events do not flow any more irreversibly back into the past. Since they have become recallable, they are always there exactly in the same sense in which believers

---

⁹ Nominalization amounts to categorization; it marks the step from natural language to conceptual thinking and, in this case, we are dealing not with material concepts but with formal categories, or, to be more precise, not with abstractive concepts but with categories proper, like *selfness*, resulting not from abstraction but from formalization. See Husserl in *Jahrbuch für Philosophie und phänomenologische Forschung* §13, "Generalisierung und Formalisierung."

can recall their original pact with the divinity.[10] As to any practical purpose, anybody *knows* that we can access any electrically mediated event through the web wherever we are and, besides, that we can recall the event whenever we want. Such very basic but embracing *knowledge* is a cognitive pattern; it guides the relationship of any person to the new media. This means that anyone is under the pressure of compressional character since everybody *knows* that what he says or does can appear on Youtube, Facebook, or an e-version of a newspaper, etc.

Compassionality is the form of sensibility fostered by the sensory and emotive character of the electrically mediated experience. Experience is by definition always concrete, that is, sensory, and as such *it triggers emotions in real time*—that is the form of coexistence with whatever thing or event one experiences—in a way that concepts and memories alone cannot. Compassionality is emotiveness in real time *without any delay*, it is *pure reaction*, and it is also compressional in the sense that distance does not matter as, for example, in the case of the drowned boy Aslan on a beach in Turkey: millions of people all over the world commiserated with the boy even if they had no clue where the corpse was and when exactly the image was captured. Compassionality is thus a form of experience "pervading" any event to which the beholder has access. It is a cognitive pattern configuring in principle all our electrically mediated experiences: one reacts emotively simply because one sees and hears. That is the reason that McLuhan refers to a "heightened human awareness of responsibility to an intense degree" (*Understanding Media* 5). He also formulates the same idea by saying that "[i]n the electric age we wear all mankind as our skin" (*Understanding Media* 47) or—albeit in a less concentrated and less metaphorical way—that, [i]n the electric age, when our central nervous system is technologically extended to involve us in the whole of mankind and to incorporate the whole of mankind in us, we necessarily *participate, in depth*, in the consequences of our every action. It is no longer possible to adopt the aloof and dissociated role of the literate Westerner. (*Understanding Media* 4)

Compassionality is the form of experience that makes one *instantly* concerned with whatever happens wherever. It amounts to a floating emotiveness readily filled up by particular emotions of sympathy or antipathy fostered by the electrically mediated things and events independently of their place of occurrence and without necessarily knowing the time of their occurrence. As a form, character, pattern, or mental set, compassionality is over-sensibility as floating emotiveness ready to be triggered with the least motive. McLuhan calls this also "involvement in depth" in the human affairs (*Understanding Media* 9).

---

[10] In general, there is no place and no time specific for doing that. Divinities are outside of space and time, so access to Divinities is neither place nor time related; it depends on faith. As to Flusser, see the German editions of *Into the Universe of Technical Images* 37 and *Towards a Philosophy of Photography* 17.

3. THE MOBILE PHONE AS ELECTRIC FORM OF EXPERIENCE

Compassionality amounts to involvement in depth in the human affairs insofar that the human affairs become by the force of electric media an indefinitely enlarged sphere of *presence* of things and events:

The *message* of the electric light [the cognitive pattern correlating with it] is like the message of electric power in industry, totally radical, pervasive, and decentralized [delocalized]. For electric light and power are separate from their uses, yet they eliminate time and space factors in human association exactly as do radio, telegraph, telephone, and TV, creating involvement in depth. (*Understanding Media* 9)

We can also say that the mediation of electric media renders us co-present with things existing and events happening everywhere and that by means of recording we become co-present with things and events of the past.[11] Distance and history have become annihilated or compressed, but by the same token, things mediatically co-present with us affect us inevitably and we become involved in depth with them. That is the effect of compressionality and compassionality.

The mobile phone intensifies the involvement in depth as floating reactive emotiveness because such involvement becomes *strictly personal*: in every experience mediated by *my* mobile phone it is *me* and just *me* who is involved, the one invoked to react as if I were directly witnessing the event—as if I were co-present with it. In watching an event in real time on TV, one is invoked to react, but TV is not personal.[12] Nevertheless, in seeing the same event on the screen of one's own mobile, one is personally invoked. One takes a stance emotively by reacting to the event shown, an event experienced by the mediation of the mobile phone as a completely personal and private gadget. One's co-presence with the event is no more accidental; it acquires the character of personal responsibility since one was looking for it in simply activating the screen of the mobile phone. As a matter of fact, McLuhan's foresight that "We are the television screen… We wear all mankind as our skin"—in the form of the aphorism given to us by Lewis Lapham in his introduction to *Understanding Media*—becomes intensely personal since we are no longer dealing with the TV as a device for relatively open access but with the very personal mobile phone screen and speakers that are exclusively ours (*Understanding Media* x). Now we *must* say: we are our mobile screen … "[w]e wear all mankind as our skin." The already personal character of our involvement, characteristic of the electric media in general, is intensified by the mobile phone because instead of finding the event casually on the impersonal TV screen, we find it using our personal screen that appeals just to us. The event *happens* on the screen of our own mobile phone and demands that we

---

[11] Following André Bazin's psychology of the photographic image, the record of the event is the event itself. See Bazin's first essay in volume 1 of *What is Cinema?* See also the section on temporal compressionality in my own "New Media and Mobile Communication" published in *Reflexiones Marginales*.

[12] Ibanez Bueno forcefully underscores the non-private character of TV: "TV is not for watching alone but for watching with someone" (25).

take a stance in *acting somehow*.[13] In using our *smartphone*, we are looking for an indefinite happening on our screen; we find what we experience on that personal screen: a call for us to take a stance for something and against somebody. That is the further *character* or pattern of what one experiences on the very personal screen, namely that something or somebody appears as victim of somebody else. The cognitive pattern or mental set fostered in this way is a moral one: one has to *react immediately* by supporting the victim and condemning the victimizer. McLuhan's "involvement in depth" develops into a floating, sentimental, irreflexive morality.

A salient point here is the further intensification of *compassionality* or involvement by compressionality. Since today more and more events are caught in the web, all of them are delocalizedly *compressed* on the web and can reach anybody any time on the screen of a mobile. The marriage of the web and the mobile phone makes the quantity of mediated experiences reaching the user of the mobile phone in real time unlimited in practical terms. The natural emotive response to what one sees and hears on the personal screen is *always* immediate, and since anything is now on the web and in real time, the *quantitative increase* of such experiences intensifies the *character of immediacy* and lack of reflection in the response to the mediated experiences. By triggering emotions immediately, without any delay, by being pure reaction, compassionality excludes reflection. The tendency to emotive reaction, i.e., to what one experiences, is always there, but the sheer amount of compressed experiences makes the reaction without reflection the *norm*. In real time, there is no time for reflection. The ruling pattern is now the tyranny of an immediate moralism.

The screen-events are an unstoppable flux precluding any reflection since every event is followed by another, so the mobile phone is the purest realization of the de-located *and* reflection-less character of the electric experience on the basis of using the personal mobile phone screen. The permanent access to de-localized experiences makes of compassionality not only a floating but a permanently active form of the experience. The *moralism* demands to support something (A) and, for this reason, to condemn somebody for hurting that something (A), becomes a permanent mental set. The mobile phone *as smartphone* is the uttermost intensification of the electric form of experience.[14] One wears all the mankind as skin permanently—as soon as one is in touch with one's own mobile, and one tends to be in touch with it always, one is also waiting just for the moment to touch one's own screen: it demands it always and we always obsequiously obey.

4. CONCLUSION. THE MOBILE PHONE AND THE ELECTRIC FORM OF THE POLITICAL: IDENTITY POLITICS

The mobile phone *as smartphone*

---

[13] Of course, we are here thinking primarily of using the mobile phone as a smartphone and of looking for news and for what is going on in social networks.

[14] Looking for news and being in social networking are not the sole functions of the *smartphone*, yet they are central activities on the smartphone.

shapes our relationships in a way that any individual or group can appear worldwide pleading for solidarity and support, demanding something and accusing somebody. That happens through the mobile phone in its capacity as a smartphone, that is through a mobile phone connected to the social networks like Facebook or Twitter and to other sources of e-news. Every receptor is invoked in real time to an immediate reaction in view of the sender's real or supposed suffering. The smartphone populates the world with supposed or real victims *and* emotionally involved observers. The *political form* generated by the structure of the experience fostered by the mobile phone as a smartphone is the union of victimism and goodism.

WORKS CITED

Bazin, André. What Is Cinema? Vol. 1. University of California Press, 2005.

Carrillo Canán, Alberto J. L. "McLuhan y las estructuras de la experiencia. El caso del alfabeto y el espacio euclidiano." Nuevo Itinerario. Revista de filosofía. No. 12, 2017, pp. 1-28.

Carrillo Canán, Alberto J. L. "Los nuevos medios y la comunicación móvil." Reflexiones Marginales. 2 June 2018, https://2018.reflexionesmarginales.com/los-nuevos-medios-y-la-comunicacion-movil/. Accessed 26 December 2018.

Flusser, Vilém. Für eine Philosophie der Fotografie, Göttingen: European Photography, 1999.

Flusser, Vilém. Ins Universum der technischen Bilder, Göttingen: European Photography, 1999.

Husserl, Edmund. Jahrbuch für Philosophie und phänomenologische Forschung, vol. 1. Halle: Max Niemeyer, 1913.

Ibanez Bueno, Jacques. Les corps commutatif: de la television à la visiophonie. Chambéry: Université Savoie Mont Blanc, 2016.

McLuhan, Marshall. The Gutenberg Galaxy. The Making of Typographic Man. University of Toronto Press, 1962.

McLuhan, Marshall. Understanding Media. The Extensions of Man. The MIT Press, 1994.

My Data Is Mine: What Is the Meaning of Participation in Data Capitalism?

João Carlos Correia
University of Beira Interior
Covilhã, Portugal

ABSTRACT: *In August 2018, several European consumer associations have launched a lawsuit against Facebook arguing that "My data is mine," but chose not to boycott the social network in its publicity campaign. The DECO FAQ list reveals why associations did not call for a boycott: they chose instead to use Facebook to disseminate information and to answer questions consumers might have. The argument presented by the associations confronts us with intricate questions concerning the nature of civil society, mainly with respect to the linkage between the market and the public sphere. Generally, critical theorists think that the realms of necessity and freedom are found incompatible with one another. The public sphere is considered as the realm of pure freedom where citizens deliberate matters concerning the destiny of the polis. The civil society is concerned with profit and with providing for material needs. The present paper approaches these questions by considering the nature of institutional configurations of contemporary digital capitalism and, also, the kind of interactions among social agents that act inside it. Are corporate digital networks (Facebook, YouTube, etc.) permeable enough to communicative rationality to make us believe that they can host a culture of convergence and cooperative interaction among social agents such that can aspire to a rational public sphere?*
To answer those queries, this paper develops a) a literature review on the contradictions of modern contemporary cognitive capitalism; b) a critical analysis of activists' statements against the use of digital networks; c) support for a critical literacy approach that identifies textual structures and contextual frameworks in digital public debate.

KEYWORDS: digital networks, Facebook, activism, critical theory, social phenomenology

1. Introduction

In August 2018, several European associations of consumers' rights from Portugal, Brazil, Belgium, Spain, and Italy have launched a lawsuit campaign against Facebook using "My data is mine" as their principal slogan. According to the statement published online by the Portuguese Association of Consumer Defense (Associação Portuguesa para a Defesa do Consumidor, popularly known under the acronym DECO), Facebook users were invited to join a class action lawsuit against the social network by signing a petition and indicating when they opened a Facebook account. Consumer associations argued that Facebook's use of its users' data should be transparent, and that consumer data should be protected by law. Therefore, promoters of the petition demanded compensation for the unauthorized use of data amounting to €200 per registered user. This average amount of recompense was calculated by economists and information experts who considered statistics provided by Facebook among other sources. In the event of a successful lawsuit or settlement, the organizers undertook to contact the petitioners and instruct them how to claim their individual compensations.[1]

According to the petition's FAQ page available on DECO's website, despite criticism of Facebook's malpractices, consumer associations that organized the petition chose not to call for a boycott of the social network on the grounds that "they also use it to disseminate information and have a page on this social network to answer the questions of consumers" ("DECO"). DECO shares with other European consumer associations a position that on several levels touches one controversial question often discussed by social theory and philosophy, namely whether and to what extent the protection of consumers' rights counts as a political right. In other words, is the protection of an individual in matters related to personal identity—of men and women as consumers of services in the context of commercial exchange—the object of political concern that should be regarded as a political right? And, what seems to be even more important, can digital social networks be considered instances of a public sphere, part of a civil society built up by an effort of democratic associations independent of political and economic power?

Consumer associations targeted Facebook with a lawsuit that objected to the use of consumers´ data as a commodity on a market-driven platform. At the same time, the associations themselves approached Facebook as an arena in civil society and a medium for critical publicity by circulating the petition's goals against the commodification of data. Significantly enough, the same digital platform where users' data was allegedly commodified was also used to denounce the process of commodification. As representatives of a consumer organization, the organizers of the petition had the mandate to support their associates as economic agents engaged in an act of consumption. Moreover, people take for granted that their rights extend to the marketplace and expect consumer rights to be protected by juridical protocols in addition to supports offered by philosophical and normative frameworks. In recognizing a link between the associative network of citizens and the activity of social actors as consumers, we acknowledge an attitude compatible with the position that consumers' rights are public issues worthy of being defended and supported in the public arena. Consequently, we adopt a hypothesis that changes in communication practices brought on by capitalist developments are never unilateral or unidimensional. Every new opportunity of communication and expansion of the market is also an opportunity for the emergence of new regimes of domination as well as an opportunity for recognition of new

---

[1] "Facebook--Já Entregámos a Ação em Tribunal." *DECO Proteste*, www.deco.proteste.pt/acoes-coletivas/os-meus-dados-sao-meus. Accessed 9 January 2019. Subsequent references to web pages on the *DECO Proteste* website will be keyed to the first word in the page title as it is listed in works cited, e.g.: "Facebook."

rights. The current technological revolution is the present stage for those contradictory claims.

2. THE MARKET, CIVIL SOCIETY, AND THE PUBLIC SPHERE

At this starting point, one is confronted with questions concerning the relationship between the market, the public sphere, and the civil society. The history of the concept of civil society oscillates between alternative perspectives. The first one tends to reduce civil society to a sphere of antagonism and irrationality, which must be subject to an external constraint for cooperation. Following the arguments of G. W. F. Hegel in *Elements of the Philosophy of Right* (1/1831/1997), Karl Marx in *The Communist Manifesto* (1848/1963), and, more recently, Hannah Arendt in *The Human Condition* (1958/1987), the realm of economic necessity and the realm of freedom are thought to be incompatible with one another.

The Hegelian effort to theorize civil society in the *Elements of the Philosophy of Right* regards it as a bourgeois society opposed to the *polis*. Civil society is a universe of autonomous individuals who establish relationships with other independent individuals based on the principle of utility and economic interest (Hegel 206). But if individual consumers act to maximize their selfish individual interests, should they be considered rational citizens? To confront the proliferation of pathologies resulting from the selfish nature of individuals—the multiplication of desires, inequality, and misery—Hegel emphasizes the rationality of the State against the hegemony of arbitrariness and particularism characteristic of civil society (Hegel 251).

The Marxist perspective, owing very much to Hegel, presents the civil society as an instance of economic (class) structures of selectivity and domination (Marx 162). Generally, Marxism identifies class relations and interests as the key to contemporary forms of collective action. According to most determinist views, the legal, associational, cultural, and public spheres of society have no independent theoretical place in Marxist analysis.

Even if one does not share what Seyla Benhabib identifies in *The Reluctant Modernism of Hannah Arendt* (1996) as the standard view of Arendt as a political philosopher of nostalgia, one must admit that Arendt searches for a lost distinction between the public and the private (Benhabib 11). Arendt's perspective, based on the Greek public sphere, criticizes the modern civil society in the context of "the rise of the social" and charges it with an increasing emphasis on the security of citizens at the expense of their concern with the common good of the *polis* (38). Benhabib claims that in Arendt's account, the social is meant as "a form of glorified national housekeeping in economic and pecuniary matters" that "displaces the concern with the political" kernel of the republic (23). Furthermore, Benhabib continues, Arendt's "social is the perfect medium in which bureaucracy, the 'rule by nobody,' emerges and unfolds" (23).

Arendt's *The Human Condition* finds modern civil society marked by the urgency of social needs at the expense of political freedom. It is understood as the development of an economic activity governed by the exchange of goods and the satisfaction of individual economic interests. The expansion of the social sphere means the disappearance of a universal and common concern for political association and citizenship from, as Benhabib puts it, "the hearts and the minds of men" (23). The political sphere becomes a pseudo-space of interaction in which individuals no longer act politically but only react as economic producers and consumers (Arendt 74). The new order shifts from values that emphasize the freedom to think and act for the public good to those that promote the security (pax) of citizens. Moderns no longer ask, as the ancients did, about the moral principles of the good life but about the factual conditions of survival. Arendt's argument raises the question whether economic freedom is really freedom or just selfish self-preservation. When one chooses the second hypothesis, it is difficult to imagine the struggle for consumer rights as real political participation.

A range of multi-dimensional perspectives on deliberative democracy and discourse theory is offered in the work of Jürgen Habermas from *The Structural Transformation of the Public Sphere* (1962/1982) to *Between Facts and Norms* (1992/1996) and in Jean L. Cohen and Andrew Arato's *Civil Society and Political Theory* (1992/2001). Those are examples of a theoretical attempt to approach civil society as the center of a political and social theory that involves a three-part critical model distinguishing civil society from both state and economy.

Following this alternative theoretical perspective, thinkers like Habermas in *The Structural Transformation of the Public Sphere* (1989) found opportunities for connecting the civil society with the public sphere: the advent of capitalist modernity should be considered an opportunity for emancipation movements as much as for the emergence of new ways of domination and reification of social relationships. The economic emergence of the new middle classes is at the kernel of the appearance of a literary and political public sphere. As Habermas observes, the elements of a new social order were taking shape with the emergence of early finance and trade capitalism: "The conditions under which the economic activity now took place lay outside of the confines of the single household; for the first time, they were of general interest" (Habermas 19). Although the moment of the constitution of the public is presented as a relatively fleeting ideal frustrated by the conditions of developing capitalism, the normative potentialities of the Enlightenment recognized by Habermas are a clear novelty compared to the implied rejection of any illusions regarding the liberal and democratic state implicit in the Hegelian and Marxist critical views.

Even in Habermas's earlier work, this clear novelty consisting of the normative ideal issuing from the rise of an enlightened public sphere has its ground in the very conditions of bourgeois life, namely in the economic changes that arise with the emergence of capitalism:

The fully developed bourgeois public sphere was based on the fictious identity of the two roles assumed by privatized individuals who came together to form a public the role of property owners and the role of human beings pure and simple. (Habermas 56)

The public sphere of citizens emerges as a functional element of the political realm assuming the normative status of " an organ for the self-articulation of the civil society with a state corresponding to his needs" (Habermas 74). Deepening this perspective, the recent problematization of civil society is understood as related to the struggle for the recognition of new issues and rights by groups that fight to obtain recognition or to affirm their visibility. Following this approach, the civil society is no more identified with the realm of needs, where social agents fight for individual maximization of profits and benefits, but, instead, *Civil Society and Political Theory* focuses "precisely on new, generally non-class-based forms of collective action oriented and linked to the legal, associational, and public institutions of society. These are differentiated not only from the state but also from the capitalist market economy" (Cohen and Arato 2). In fact, a significant part of the configuration of modern civil societies is due to the energies of groups such as religious movements, trade unions, anti-precarity movements, as well as movements spearheaded by migrants' rights, consumer rights, and environmental associations. These movements use new discursive practices to emphasize the principle of plurality and the consequent recognition of new agendas and new social and collective identities that have emerged in the consolidation of modernity.

3. THE DIGITAL CAGE

Those approaches must be simultaneously confronted and articulated with institutional configurations of contemporary digital capitalism and, also, by means of interactions among social agents that act inside those configurations.

If one believes in the relative autonomy of the associative civil society from the political and economic systems, the question that arises next, in the current case, is whether the digital networks owned by corporations like Facebook or YouTube are permeable to alternative rationality that implies the kind of cooperative interaction among social agents that Habermas would expect not from a system but in a lifeworld. This is a hypothesis that we can embrace with the clarification that our concept of the lifeworld preserves from Habermas's *Lebenswelt* the rule of discourse and ordinary language and the cooperative nature of interactions but does not accept that those are its only features. Lifeworld, as we see it, is not an essentialist instance of cooperation opposed to systemic reality but a place where one finds several uses of language (including the strategic one) and several domains of meaning, some of them marked by reification and dominance. The tension that a lifeworld preserves within helps to stave off the hegemony of a systemic rationality.

Or, instead, are the so-called institutions of cooperative interaction just profit-driven devices owned by giant corporations that turn shared information and social interactions among social actors into commodities? Is it possible to see citizens as consumers and vice-versa? Is participation on Facebook a *de facto* commodification of audiences or should we recognize the implicit contradictions of cognitive capitalism and consider Facebook, as the consumer associations do, interesting enough to develop movements independent of the economic and political system? We saw in the public statement in which DECO dissuaded users from a boycott that consumer associations do not agree with the determinist point of view that sees information and communication technologies (ICT) and digital networks as corporate gadgets driven to data gathering and turning the audiences into commodities sold to advertisers. Our guiding questions resurface at last: may the digital networks work as a sphere of democratic and political participation? Will digital media be able to perform this role and turn passive audiences into active publics?

Following the concept of an open civil society in *Between Facts and Norms* (1992/1996), the public sphere is seen as a sphere of identification and detection of problems whose influence should continue to be reflected in the subsequent treatment of the issues that take place within the political system (359). Following this suggestion, many supporters of the democratic role of the Internet believe that a democratic and open political system is empowered by the autonomous activity of formation of public opinion, which can be carried by citizens' movements, social movements, and political participation nourished by social networks.

On the other hand, we have the institutional and legislative process that culminates in decisions that concern the development of concrete policies and legislative outputs. The Internet may be compared to a resonance box that amplifies the pressure of problems by dramatizing them, so they are considered by the parliamentary institutions. Thus, the identification of issues in the public sphere (civil rights, feminism, consumers' rights) usually follows the route designed by Habermas in *Between Facts and Norms*: (i) the issues are raised by intellectuals and social activists in the periphery of the political system; (ii) they are then picked up by journals, associations, clubs, forums for citizens, universities, professional organizations, social networks and so on; (iii) the issues crystallize at the heart of social movements and subcultures; (iv) they enter into the public agenda, reach a wide audience, and ultimately influence policy makers and legislative institutions (341–342).

There are several reasons to devise alternative ways of communication such as online movements that support popular petitions—a practice very popular in Portugal. Those alternative ways of communication emphasize a dynamic relationship with social movements, a relationship that maintains itself open to critical attitude and to the interchange of knowledge, opinions, feelings, and arguments. From this point of view, despite being traditionally confined by elitist and neoliberal theories to the private domain (women's rights, domestic violence, identitarian claims), elements of domination current in the lifeworld become issues of a critical debate in an open and independent civil society. Acknowledging those opportunities, we embrace a critical perspective conceptually influenced by authors such as Christian Fuchs and Vincent Mosco in their collaboration on *Marx in the Age of Digital Capitalism* and maintain that one must not ignore the other side of the use of social platforms that minimizes this participatory and democratic view.

In the contemporary digital landscape, the prosumers, a neologism coined by Alvin Toffler in his book *The Third Wave* (1980) create, without reward, value for the products of entrepreneurs who provide them with content production. As Fuchs and Mosco ask, will the logic of shared content production recognize users only as creators of the products marketed by the corporations that control the platform or will they become the beneficiaries of the sharing of information and knowledge? (10) Will the prosumers be not only the unpaid producers but also the merchandise as audiences, clicks, and views that are essential for advertising on social networking platforms? If the data is used by Facebook for profit, are not the users and the content produced by them turned into commodities?

At the strictly political level, social networks are also suspected of reviving premodern elements. The irrationalism resulting from the exacerbation of affections coexists with the world of instant messages, direct television, inflamed tweets, and media controversies that seems to reinforce the commodified nature of such political participation. If one finds that social networks exploit free labor by using participation to gather data while commodifying and tribalizing audiences, it is difficult to see participation on social networking platforms as something that configures a new participatory dynamic performed by an enlightened public. In the reified environment of public media of communication, political participation rarely meets the strong demands of authentic political freedom posited in the pure public sphere by Habermas and Arendt.

However, in the end, one finds an expansion of opportunities for critical agency. There is not any real and concrete experience of media democratization that fully fulfils the requirements of an ideal-type public sphere or any configuration of free and participatory communicative experience as envisioned by Walter Benjamin in "The Work of Art in the Age of Its Technological Reproducibility" (1936/1987, 196) as there is no "iron cage" like the one designed by Adorno and Horkheimer in their seminal essay, "The Enlightenment as Mass Deception" originally published in *Dialectic of Enlightenment* (1944/1995, 163).

The technological determinism visible both in orthodox Marxism and Fordist industrial capitalism is unable to explain the complexity of technological practices because it sees them only in an instrumental way and forgets their nature as social phenomena. But a utopia founded in a technological determinism also falls short of explaining the contradictions of collective participation. Postmodernism, for instance, has been based on cultural fetishism that dissolved the conflicts of economy and class into the realm of symbols, culture, and signification. On the other hand, orthodox Marxist approaches reduce life to labor. One fetishizes labor, the other fetishizes symbols, as Fuchs argues in *Critical Theory of Communication* (48). If techno-libertarian and some postmodern ideologies fetishize digital games and symbols under the theoretical umbrella of a creative self, orthodox critics on their side are unable to understand the nature of tensions between participation and consumption.

Critical Internet Studies are now getting support and attention. Many collectives of participatory nature (MoveOn.org; platforms tailored to the needs of older consumers like https://www.age-platform.eu/policy-work/consumer-rights; or platforms dedicated to a particular commodity like Dona Ana Mutual Domestic Water Consumers Association Privacy Policies at https://www.dawater.org/privacy.htm) are successful in pursuing alternative models in raising new policy and regulatory challenges, including consumer protection issues. Regulation and use of software platforms that require a user profile and collect identificatory data are now studied and analyzed in emerging fields of sociological attention. These studies emphasize the need for a deconstruction of the techno-libertarian hegemony, debates on software ownership regimes, attention to corporate risks, digital divide, surveillance, development of sustainable and innovative economic models, and critical literacy directed to the use of online platforms that track users' data. In this particular sense, a perspective that distinguishes between public and private but does not account for the ever more pressing problems of consumers' rights will be too narrow for the understanding of many of the emergent political challenges.

WORKS CITED

Adorno, Theodor, and Max Horkheimer. "The Culture Industry: Enlightenment in Mass Deception." *Dialectic of Enlightenment.* Verso, 1995, pp. 120-167. (*Dialektik der Aufklärung*, 1944).

Arendt, Hannah. *The Human Condition.* Chicago University Press, 1987.

Benhabib, Seyla. *The Reluctant Modernism of Hannah Arendt.* Rowman & Littlefield, 2000.

Benjamin, Walter, "A Obra de Arte na Era da Sua Reprodutibilidade Técnica" in *Obras Escolhidas: Magia e Técnica, Arte e Política.* São Paulo: Editora Brasiliense, 1987, pp. 165-19. (*Das Kunstwerk im Zeitalter seiner Technischen Reproduzierbarkeit/The Work of Art in the Age of Its Technological Reproducibility*, 1936).

Cohen, Jean L., and Andrew Arato. *Civil Society and Political Theory.* The MIT Press, 2001.

"DECO Leva Facebook a Tribunal." *DECO Proteste*, www.deco.proteste.pt/tecnologia/tablets-computadores/noticias/deco-leva-facebook-a-tribunal#. Accessed 9 January 2019.

Fuchs, Christian. *Critical Theory of Communication: New Readings of Lukács, Adorno, Marcuse, Honneth, and Habermas in the Age of the Internet.* University of Westminster Press, 2016.

Fuchs, Christian, and Vincent Mosco, editors. *Marx in the Age of Digital Capitalism.* Studies in Critical Social Sciences, edited by David Fasenfest, Volume 80. Leiden: Brill, 2016.

Habermas, Jürgen. *The Structural Transformation of the Public Sphere: An Inquiry into a Category of Bourgeois Society*, The MIT Press, 1989. (*Strukturwandel der Öffenstlichkeit*, 1962).

Habermas, Jürgen. *Between Facts and Norms*. The MIT Press, 1996. (*Faktizität und Geltung. Beitragë zur Diskurstheorie des Rechts und des demokratischen Rechsstaats*, 1992)

Hegel, Georg Wilhelm Friedrich. *Principes de la Philosophie du Droit*. Paris, Gallimard, 1997. (*Grundlinien der Philosophie des Rechts,* 1831).

Marx, Karl. *Œuvres I - Économie I*, Bibliothèque de la Pléiade, Gallimard, 1963. (*Manifest der Kommunistischen Partei*, 1848).

Toffler, Alvin. *The Third Wave*. Bantham Books, 1980.

Global Media Literacy: A Conceptual Error and Eight Typologies

ULAŞ BAŞAR GEZGIN

DUY TAN UNIVERSITY
DANANG, VIETNAM

ABSTRACT: *In this theoretical article, we identify a conceptual error in the notion of 'global media literacy' and present and discuss eight typologies of media literacy formed on the basis of the ideological, political and economic dimensions of media and media literacy. While the first four types (Types 1-4) are past-oriented, they differ in terms of their endorsement or criticism of the government and capitalism. The same holds for the remaining four types (Types 5-8) except with respect to their future orientations. The time orientation, attitudes towards the government and capitalism determine how media literacy is conceptualized and what type of media literacy is to be promoted. It is proposed that unlike the original sense of literacy which was cognitively based, media literacy is socially constructed, which means that the widespread literacy analogy drawn from reading and writing to media use and interpretation is problematic. Finally, after delineating the eight typologies of media literacy, we discuss whether they apply to the digital world. It is argued that Type 8 media which is future-oriented, anti-government, and anti-capitalist find opportunities in the digital world which they lack due to funding issues in the non-digital world. Another point of the discussion involves the less tribal nature of digital media use since digital media users have access to different views which is not always the case for users of non-digital media. It is hoped that the typology of media literacy presented in this article will be critically discussed and utilized in future studies in the field.*

KEYWORDS: literacy, media literacy, pro-government vs. anti-government orientation, pro-capitalist vs. anti-capitalist orientation, and past-orientation vs. future-orientation.

1. INTRODUCTION

Media literacy is one of the buzzwords of our times. Justin Lewis and Sut Jhally report that the concept was used initially in building critical models of citizenship (109), but media literacy nowadays is in favor with surprisingly diverse groups of people, movements, and interests ranging from liberals on the left to religious conservatives on the right. Critical thinkers promote media literacy to guard people against corporate or government deception while religious conservatives turn to media literacy to protect their children and the youth from the moral corruption of the media. It is surprising to see that people holding different points of view come up with media literacy as a solution to their problems. Whether their solutions are indeed the same now needs some clarification. A confusion arises from the fact that the notion of media literacy is ill-conceived from the very beginning.

The term literacy makes perfect sense: we can learn and teach others how to read and write. It is possible for literacy rate to be 100% in a country, as exemplified by Finland (Miller and McKenna 23). We propose in this paper to define literacy in terms of cognitive ability and maintain that social factors have a negligible impact on that ability.[1] In support of this position, we observe that people can have different world views, life styles, habits, attitudes, but still be literate. Nevertheless, the variables just mentioned are differentially influential for the notion of media literacy and affect whether various groups of people can be deemed media-literate and to what extent. The analogy fails, as literacy pertains to cognition and media literacy to the social world. The notion of media literacy refers to critical thinking skills applied to media, but what counts as critical thinking depends on ideological, political, and economic dimensions of media and the citizens. A conspiracy theory blaming ethnic and religious groups for social problems passes for 'critical' in certain contexts, as an alternative account of the social affairs, but in another setting such a view is deemed unrealistic, racist, and discriminatory. Likewise, conspiracy theories can be criticized as they turn out to be not critical enough. For instance, there may be a tendency to criticize American foreign policy but not capitalism. Foreign policy can be criticized as if it were independent of underlying capitalistic motives. Such a position will be less critical than an anti-capitalist stance. If that is the case, we need to identify the ideological, political, and economic dimensions of media literacy. Table 1 shows the dimensions and typologies emerging from their intersections. It is necessary to acknowledge at this point that our schematization of social facts consists of simplified versions of reality. Thus, this typology of media should be viewed as a tentative theoretical model rather than an empirical study.

TABLE 1:
EIGHT TYPOLOGIES OF MEDIA LITERACY

	Ideological Dimension	Political Dimension	Economic Dimension
1	Past-oriented	Pro-government	Pro-capitalist
2	Past-oriented	Pro-government	Anti-capitalist
3	Past-oriented	Anti-government	Pro-capitalist
4	Past-oriented	Anti-government	Anti-capitalist
5	Future-oriented	Pro-government	Pro-capitalist
6	Future-oriented	Pro-government	Anti-capitalist
7	Future-oriented	Anti-government	Pro-capitalist
8	Future-oriented	Anti-government	Anti-capitalist

2. EIGHT TYPES OF MEDIA

Past-oriented media intentionalities and contents are those that refer to and celebrate a golden era in the past. According to them, the world should be reorganized based on sacred principles or traditions. The most typical examples of this type are religious fundamentalism and nationalism. In contrast, a future-orientation embraces a belief in

---

[1] Here we are not making country-level comparisons. However, a comparison will show that common sense, which assumes a necessary relationship between literacy rates and economic development, is not true. The largest economies of the world (e.g. the United States and China) do not have the highest literacy rates. They rank behind less affluent countries. Likewise, North Korea, while not a high-income country, is among the countries with the highest literacy rates (UNESCO 453).

democracy and progress in science. Democracy is future-oriented as it is continuously evolving. People who have been excluded, for example on the basis of color, gender, or sexual orientation, are now recognized. Science is also future-oriented in its foundational belief that every new discovery will improve on the previous ones. Of course, due to the rise of anti-democratic movements like technocracy, theocracy, or oligarchy, etc., democracy can become a phenomenon of the past, but this does not affect our main idea here that democracy is a hope for the future, not a nostalgia. Whereas the past is perceived as dogmatic, outdated, and primitive, the democratic lens views future as full of hopes and dreams. The orientations toward past and future clearly differ in their media intentionalities and contents as the former addresses itself to the splendor of the past and tries to convince the audience that life was better in the past despite all the difficulties.

There are pro-government and anti-government media. We also add the axis of pro-capitalism vs. anti-capitalism because not all the anti-government media are anti-capitalist. Political polarization on the one hand and corporate mergers and acquisitions on the other make middle positions untenable for mainstream media. That is because political and economic polarizations force media corporations to take sides. Furthermore, as Marxist theory explains, capitalism has the tendency to monopolize in the long term. Against the 'too-big-to-fail' corporate players, small companies have very low chances of survival (Brewer 20). Scholars like Christopher Hanretty and Catie Baillard, who write about the effects of corporate media on politics, suggest that most media are in fact the voice of the boss (Hanretty 335, Bailard 583). If this is true, then we may well expect alternative media to be future-oriented, anti-government and anti-capitalist (i.e., Type 8). From an intellectual point of view, all media should be subjected to critical thinking. The past-oriented types can ask for media literacy to resist the ideology promoted by the future-oriented types and vice versa. The past-oriented media can claim that children exposed to future-oriented media do not learn their history, forget their religious roots, and/or have weaker ties with their nation and its state. Same conflict holds for anti-government media against pro-government media and vice versa. Anti-government media may claim that the indoctrination of pro-government media viewers reproduces the current status quo. To cope with the brainwashing of the government media, anti-government media audiences would demand media literacy. In the other direction, the pro-government circles can ask for media literacy as the other media, according to them, are just doing ideological anti-propaganda against the state. Furthermore, the media and its contents may reflect the voice of who owns them as stated above (Bailard 583). This third possibility is what we should reform in a democratic society. In his monumental study of media ownership around the world, *Who Owns the World's Media*, Eli Noam demonstrates that top companies often own media as a 'side dish' along with their main business activities (1180). Not only does a media outlet bring prestige to the company, but also a channel to convey its corporate propaganda. The ties between the company and the media are usually concealed to claim the objectivity of the news, programming, and publications. Justin Schlosberg's *Media Ownership and Agenda Control* published in the same year as *Who Owns the World's Media* supports Noam's claim that it is rare to have a large company not owned by a top company in other business areas (116). Since these relationships are usually concealed, it should be the task of media literacy advocates to reveal the hidden structure of ownership.

For examples of media types 1-4, we can look at Christian evangelical, Muslim fundamentalist, or nationalistic TV stations (Eisenlohr 869). Type 1 media, which is past-oriented, pro-government, and pro-capitalist, is the most common. This is also the most authoritarian form of media that promotes the old-age norms of obedience, compliance, and conformity. Its followers conceptualize the world as if they lived in the golden age defined by religion or national history. They support the markets as the most widespread world order. We may question how market demands on the media would be aligned with those posed by religion or tradition or we can object that market demands would be corrosive to the other two, but, in reality, capitalism and religion often support each other in the name of neo-liberalism coupled with religious conservatism. For instance, anthropology scholars Jon Bialecki, Naomi Haynes, and Joel Robbins critically discuss the intricate links between Christianity and capitalism and illuminate some of the less visible connections (1150). In countries such as Turkey or the wealthy Arab states, the church or other religious establishments promote capitalism and are in favor of neo-liberal policies (Adas 113).[2] According to Type 1 media, the present-day social problems such as high crime rate, poverty, unemployment, etc., surge when people do not follow religion, remember the glory of their nation, or obey their state. Blaming the victim (Wright 1), just world hypothesis (Furnham 795), scapegoating (Bullock 229), and moral panic (Hunt 629) are all characteristic of Type 1 media.

Type 2 media, which is past-oriented, pro-government, and anti-capitalist, resembles Type 1 but does not support capitalism. Instead, it may celebrate the value of feudalism, for example. It sends the message that people were happier before capitalism. This type corresponds to the recent shift in Vatican's official discourse (Ferrara 42). The endorsement of feudalism distinguishes Type 2 from Type 4, which is past-oriented, anti-government, and anti-capitalist and corresponds to Latin American liberation theology. We mention Latin American liberation theology and not Latin American liberation philosophy in general, because the former is based on religion and, therefore, past-oriented. Unlike Type 1, Type 2 rejects the idea that our social problems can be attributed to God and understands them to be man-made. Man-made problems can be fixed without the

---

[2] It may be surprising to see that a past-oriented model can also be pro-capitalist. Capitalism is not a new mode of production. It has around two centuries of history (Hussain xxv).

intervention of God, but Type 2 media present solutions that do not look ahead of capitalism, but back to feudal times we picked as an example for this type.

Type 3 media, which is past-oriented, anti-government, and pro-capitalist, resembles Type 1 and Type 2 only in their commendation of the nation, religion, and history, but disagrees about the role of government in capitalism. Type 3 supports capitalism and blames the government for not doing enough for paving the way for capitalism in terms of deregulating markets, privatizing public enterprises, and lowering taxes (Tabrizi 1922). Assuming that social ills are man-made, Type 3 presents capitalism as the cure for all our problems.

Type 4 is past-oriented, anti-government, and anti-capitalist. As already indicated, it roughly corresponds to Latin American liberation theology. This type of media correctly realizes that our social problems are man-made rather than God-made. Capitalism is not the cure, but the disease; the government represents the oppressors, and dominant classes are responsible for social evils. However, the ideas disseminated by this type of media still fall under the influence of religious beliefs. While reforming their epistemic origin, they are still bound by the mythic narratives of the religious past.[3]

Type 5 media is future-oriented, pro-government, and pro-capitalist. Its followers believe that in order to progress in the future, they have to implement capitalism and obey the government unconditionally and unquestioningly. It looks like a quasi-modern view in its emphasis on progress, while it differs from Type 1 media through the ideological dimension, i.e. the time orientation. A nationalist state with progress as its key motivation fits Type 5.

Type 6 media are future-oriented, pro-government, and anti-capitalist. They attract followers who believe in future progress, criticize capitalism, but, at the same time, support the government. These are often media operating in socialist countries or countries with socialist heritage such as Cuba.

Type 7 media are future-oriented, anti-government, and pro-capitalist and match some of the anti-government media in socialist countries or countries with socialist heritage. They believe in progress, but they think this is possible with the implementation of capitalism, and thus they are against the government which does not support or sufficiently support capitalism.

Finally, Type 8 is future-oriented, anti-government, and anti-capitalist and describes most dissident media in capitalist countries. Similar to Type 4, which is past-oriented, anti-government, and anti-capitalist, Type 8 media analyzes the misdeeds of capitalism and the government's role in these. They believe in progress, but they do not think it is possible with the current government and its capitalist economy to move ahead.

We have described eight types of media according to the criteria we

---

[3] Although the past is not necessarily religious, the religions necessarily refer to the past.

propose to be the most relevant for the identification of different forms of media literacy. Our typology shows that the demands for media literacy would be different for different types of media and that is why a monolithic understanding of the notion of media literacy is untenable. Before we move to the next discussion, let us express a few reservations about this model in addition to our initial disclaimer. First, this triadic attempt to delineate the characteristics of media falters in cases where the media—sports newspapers, for example—do not fit any type because of their unclear ideological, political and/or economic positions (English 1001). Second, this typology can be extended by adding new categories which will result in 16 types for 4 binary categories, 32 types for 5 binary categories, 2^n for n categories, etc. For example, we can follow Mari K. Niemi and Ville Pitkänen and add gender bias as an analytical dimension of media literacy (355). Or, we could construct egalitarian and patriarchal versions of the eight types analyzed here. In this article, we limit ourselves to three categories for the sake of conceptual clarity. Now, we can move to the next discussion, which is about the digital world.

3. Applicability of the Eight Types Model to the Digital World

Of course, the digital realm has its peculiar characteristics, but as a starting point of discussion, we need to take note of the fact that all the main media corporations of the non-digital realm are also active in the digital realm with their portals, websites, social media accounts etc. That means the digital realm is not completely independent of the non-digital realm. However, the ownership structure of the non-digital realm differs from that of the digital realm to some extent.

Let us reinterpret our model in terms of ownership distribution to clarify this point. In the realm of non-digital media, the most common forms of media are pro-government and pro-capitalist. In case of the anti-government media, the funder is either a member of the wealthy class who is not content with government policies, a political organization like a party or a trade union, or an international special interests' group. While the pro-government media can take advantage of enormous public resources for their benefit, the resources of a wealthy individual or an organization are limited. Anti-capitalist media are quite rare in non-digital realm because they have even fewer funding options than the anti-government media. A member of a wealthy class can fund anti-government media to promote his class interests, but rare is the scenario—and characterized by cognitive and social dissonance—in which the class position of an individual is in conflict with the class interests promoted by the anti-capitalist media funded by him. The only funding option for Type 8 media (future-oriented, anti-government, and anti-capitalist) is through grassroots organizations which are almost never as strong as the governments or the wealthiest classes. This means Type 1 (past-oriented, pro-government, and pro-capitalist) and Type 5 (future-oriented, pro-government, and pro-capitalist) are the mostly likely types of media as long as media requires investment of capital whereas Type 8 will be the least likely one. Type 4 media (past-oriented, anti-government, and anti-capitalist) is largely enabled by the support of a religious community in non-digital life.

As a result of increasing Internet accessibility and the expansion of information and communication technologies, Type 8 media have found new opportunities in the digital world. Some Type 8 media can reach a larger audience on the net than by means of non-digital media even though their operations may be banned or restricted by the authorities (Hintz 325). Thus, except the difference in circulation, digital media literacy relies on the same typologies.

This is not the whole story, however. Medium- to large-scale funding is necessary for establishing and operating media in the non-digital realm, but there are many low-cost options to run media operations in the digital world. That is why, in addition to the eight types, we have non-corporate and non-institutional media sources in the digital world. Nevertheless, after a closer look, we will see that these sources, as well as their corresponding users, can be accommodated by these eight categories. For example, some of the social media users will be more anti-government, less past-oriented, more anti-capitalist (i.e. Type 8 user) compared to others and so match one of the media types in our model.

In addition to identifying the types of media in the digital world, we have unique challenges for media literacy in the digital world. More often than the followers of traditional media, those who prefer digital media access sources that do not necessarily fit their ideological, political, and economic beliefs. In that sense, the users of non-digital media are more tribal (Winter, Metzger, and Flanagin 685). Especially on Twitter, a typical problem pops up when politicians tweet to the public, which in terms of social psychology consists of in-group and out-group members, as if they tweeted to their confidantes (i.e. their in-groups). Similarly, newspapers in the non-digital realm may be accustomed to address their ideologically profiled news to a readership of loyal followers, but that is not the case in the digital world. In the digital world, the media are expected to be more reasonable or else they are open to virtual attacks by followers of different ideas and beliefs. Another point relevant for digital media literacy would be the effect of replication and trolling. The naive followers should be made aware that a post shared by millions of users is not necessarily true. It can be shared multiple times just for the opposite reason, that is because it is not true. Shares do not mean an endorsement. Furthermore, media followers should be careful about trolls who are not in the digital world for benevolent purposes, but for mockery, ideology, social persuasion, and even for some legally gray activities (Cruz 15).

4. Conclusion

In this article, we argued that the analogy between literacy and media literacy is not applicable because the media are not homogeneous. We noted that the confusion arises from a shared terminology, but we pointed out that literacy depends on cognitive ability that—as an ability—is fairly independent of socioeconomic variables, whereas media literacy requires different approaches for different media types on the basis of relevant ideological, political, and economic dimensions. We presented and discussed eight types of media to show how they would present different demands for media literacy. This was followed by a brief discussion of how digital media literacy would be similar and how it would differ from the traditional media. We now propose a study of media literacy conditioned by the dimensions we have outlined in the foregoing typology and resulting from the intersection of the following binary categories: past vs. future, pro-government vs. anti-government, and capitalist vs. anti-capitalist orientations. We hope that the typology proposed in this article will be useful for future studies.

WORKS CITED

Adas, Emin Baki. "The Making of Entrepreneurial Islam and the Islamic Spirit of Capitalism." *Journal for Cultural Research*, vol. 10, no. 2, 2006, pp. 113-137.

Bailard, Catie Snow. "Corporate Ownership and News Bias Revisited: Newspaper Coverage of the Supreme Court's Citizens United Ruling." *Political Communication,* vol. 33, no. 4, 2016, pp. 583-604.

Bialecki, Jon, Naomi Haynes, and Joel Robbins. "The Anthropology of Christianity." *Religion Compass*, vol. 2, no. 6, 2008, pp. 1139-1158.

Brewer, Anthony. *Marxist Theories of Imperialism: A Critical Survey*. Routledge, 2002.

Bullock, Heather E., Karen Fraser Wyche, and Wendy R. Williams. "Media Images of the Poor." *Journal of Social Issues*, vol. 57, no. 2, 2001, pp. 229-246.

Cruz, Angela Gracia B., Yuri Seo, and Mathew Rex. "Trolling in Online Communities: A Practice-Based Theoretical Perspective." *The Information Society*, vol. 34, no. 1, 2018, pp. 15-26.

Eisenlohr, Patrick. "Reconsidering Mediatization of Religion: Islamic Televangelism in India." *Media, Culture & Society*, vol. 39, no. 6, 2017, pp. 869-884.

English, Peter. "Mapping the Sports Journalism Field: Bourdieu and Broadsheet Newsrooms." *Journalism*, vol. 17, no. 8, 2016, pp. 1001-1017.

Ferrara, Pasquale. "The Concept of Periphery in Pope Francis' Discourse: A Religious Alternative to Globalization?" *Religions*, vol .6, no. 1, 2015, pp. 42-57.

Furnham, Adrian. "Belief in a Just World: Research Progress over the Past Decade." *Personality and Individual Differences*, vol. 34, no. 5, 2003, pp. 795-817.

Hanretty, Chris. "Media Outlets and Their Moguls: Why Concentrated Individual or Family Ownership is Bad for Editorial Independence." *European Journal of Communication*, vol. 29, no. 3, 2014, pp. 335-350.

Hintz, Arne. "Restricting Digital Sites of Dissent: Commercial Social Media and Free Expression." *Critical Discourse Studies*, vol. 13, no. 3, 2016, pp. 325-340.

Hunt, Arnold. "'Moral Panic' and Moral Language in the Media." *British Journal of Sociology*, vol. 48, no. 4, 1997, pp. 629-648.

Hussain, Syed B. *Encyclopedia of Capitalism*. Facts on File, Inc, 2004.

Lewis, Justin, and Sut Jhally. "The Struggle over Media Literacy."

Journal of Communication, vol. 48, no. 1, 1998, pp. 109-120.

Miller, John W., and Michael C. McKenna. *World Literacy: How Countries Rank and Why It Matters*. Routledge, 2016.

Niemi, Mari K., and Ville Pitkänen. "Gendered Use of Experts in the Media: Analysis of the Gender Gap in Finnish News Journalism." *Public Understanding of Science*, vol. 26, no. 3, 2017, pp. 355-368.

Noam, Eli M. *Who Owns the World's Media?: Media Concentration and Ownership around the World*. Oxford University Press, 2016.

Schlosberg, Justin. *Media Ownership and Agenda Control: The Hidden Limits of the Information Age*. Routledge, 2016.

Tabrizi, Sirous. "Connections between Neo-liberalism, Neo-conservatism, and Critical Democracy in Education." *International Journal for Cross-Disciplinary Subjects in Education (IJCDSE)*, vol. 4, no. 1, 2014, pp. 1922-1929.

UNESCO. *Global Education Monitoring Report: Education for People and Planet*. UNESCO, 2016. en.unesco.org/gem-report/sites/gem-report/files/GEM_Report_2016_2nd_edition_Statistical_Tables.pdf. Accessed 29 Dec. 2018.

Winter, Stephan, Miriam J. Metzger, and Andrew J. Flanagin. "Selective Use of News Cues: A Multiple-Motive Perspective on Information Selection in Social Media Environments." *Journal of Communication*, vol. 66, no. 4, 2016, pp. 669-693.

Wright, Susan E. "Presidential Address: Blaming the Victim, Blaming Society or Blaming the Discipline: Fixing Responsibility for Poverty and Homelessness." *The Sociological Quarterly*, vol. 34, no. 1, 1993, pp. 1-16.

Exploring the Digital Attitude: Where Form and Content Blur

STACEY O'NEAL IRWIN

MILLERSVILLE UNIVERSITY OF PENNSYLVANIA
MILLERSVILLE, PENNSYLVANIA, USA

ABSTRACT: *In the early days of the Internet, philosophers, consumers, engineers, and futurists wondered what Web 1.0, the initial stage of the world wide web, might look like. At the time, there was not even a space called the world wide web, let alone the moniker "Web 1.0." As the Internet flourished, consumers were spun into its sticky, silky residue. More connections and devices heralded in Web 2.0, including changes in both the form and the content of digital media. Now, with Web 3.0 right around the corner as we head into the thirtieth year of widespread web use, we explore the digital attitude adopted towards digital media in contemporary society. The idea of an attitude suggests the typical way we are feeling about a certain thing at the time. How do users and consumers and human beings in general assess their digital media use and understanding? Lines blur between where contents and forms begin and end. The digital media "content" needs a device and the "device" needs content to engage the consumer/user. Form comes through technological, electronic, digital, and device driven ways. Content proliferates through media through a variety of user generated programming, visuals, sound, apps, games, TV shows, billboards, and software. The combination of these elements provides digital media with its spreadable and participatory nature. This reflection considers the digital attitude as it relates to the human-technology experience approaching the Web 3.0 era. Does the web+digital+media's ubiquity highlight or in some way name a new or different kind of in-between and taken-for granted attitude? Ideas from of Don Ihde, Alfred Schutz and Thomas Luckman, Marshall McLuhan, and Peter-Paul Verbeek are considered.*

KEYWORDS: human-technology relations, digital media, Web 3.0, technology, mediatized

> Technologies transform our experiences of the world and our perceptions and interpretations of our world, and we in turn become transformed in the process. Transformations are non-neutral.
> --Don Ihde, *Postphenomenology and Technoscience: The Peking University Lectures*, 2009, 44.

In the early days of the Internet—in the 1970s—consumers, engineers, philosophers, and futurists wondered what Web 1.0, the initial stage of the world wide web, might look like. At the time, there was not even a space called the world wide web, let alone the moniker "Web 1.0." As the Internet flourished, humans were spun into its sticky, silky residue. The world was transformed. In the years after Web 1.0, more connections and devices heralded in Web 2.0, which included the form and content of digital media. In this somewhat amorphous era, there was a central shift to the way digital content was created, shared, stored, spread, and used. Now, with Web 3.0 right around the corner, and as we head into the thirtieth year of widespread web use, I wonder, what is the *digital attitude* that has been widely adopted and continually expanding towards digital media in contemporary society? In what ways has humanity been transformed?

Digital media and Internet connection are closely linked partners in the mediated world. The content needs a device and the device needs content to engage the consumer/user. Content is digitally formed and comes through technological, electronic, digital, and device driven ways, proliferating through user generated programming, visuals, sound, apps, games, TV shows, billboards, and software. Lines blur between where content and form begin and end. The combination provides digital media with a spreadable and participatory nature. This short reflection considers the digital attitude, the human-technology experience of using digital media in our connected culture in the forthcoming Web 3.0 era. Does the web+digital+media ubiquity highlight or in some way name a new or different kind of in-between and taken-for-granted attitude through its use? Merleau-Ponty (1969), Schütz and Luckman (1973), Hasse (2008), and Ihde (1990, 2009) contemplate the taken-for-granted experience of using digital technologies, while Van Den Eede (2011), Rosenberger and Verbeek (2015), and others name and explore the in-between of digitally mediated experience in our world. McLuhan (1964) explores symbiosis of form and content. When considered together, they highlight important concepts of the digital attitude in the World Wide Web era.

Getting to Web 3.0

It seems important at this juncture, to review how we have become entangled in this highly technologized world. Historians like David Millard and Martin Ross look at many different points that mark the beginning of what we might call the technological revolution. The first stage is the Web 1.0 era, which is generally described as the use of static websites without interactive content. The read-only web content connects information from the larger websphere. The next stage, Web 2.0, shifts the focus to a more interactive and open website architecture, design, and execution—like the read-write web that connects people within the Internet through hypertext. Next, Web 3.0 combines read-write-execute web that connects knowledge hubs and clouds and sifts the content for information to merge and connect (Millard and Ross 27-30). This is where we are currently poised within the web continuum in the first quarter of the new millennium.

The ability to connect individual habits and attitudes through data, to complete semantic searching to cull and discern meaning from the data, to create knowledge bases from key words to algorithms, and to limit complexity and organize information into problems by building new ontologies opens doors to increasingly interesting and important topics like ethics, privacy, and security. Personal Intelligent Digital Assistants like Siri, Echo, Nina, and Cortana, as well as a select few social robots, proliferate in this contemporary environment. In this Web 3.0 zone, the digital attitude addresses NOT our attitude about digital technologies, but the problem of HOW technologies use data to analyze our attitudinal mindset on everything from preferences to values and habits discernible from the data we provide through use. This entangled connection has been occurring since the 1990s, but the new abilities are not just persuasive but specifically aimed at forging new habits in ways beyond fitness and lifestyle choices.

It is important to consider that in this Web 3.0 environment, technologies are transforming our experiences, perceptions, and interpretations of our world and we are increasingly transformed in the process. Web 3.0 facilitates and is facilitated by digital media. This blend of form and content is composed of three parts that distinguish them from previous media forms, namely content, channel, and application. Henry Jenkins, Joshua Green, and Sam Ford explain the importance of this change in *Spreadable Media: Creating Value and Meaning in a Networked Culture*: "This shift from distribution to circulation signals a movement toward a more participatory model of culture, one which sees the public not as simply consumers of preconstructed messages but as people who are shaping, sharing, reframing, and remixing media content in ways which might not have been previously imagined" (2). Lines blur between where content and form begin and end. The digital media content needs the device and the device needs the content to engage the consumer/user. Form comes through technological, electronic, digital and device driven ways. Content proliferates through digital media, a variety of user generated programming, visuals and sound, apps, games, TV shows, billboards, and software. The combination of all of these elements provides digital media with the spreadable and participatory nature. All-together, the in-between of the human-technology relations and the intermediary place of the technology, create Web 3.0.

BEING IN THE MIDST

A variety of scholars have explored the in-between of digital media and the human-technology relations. Don Ihde names the feeling of being between, among, or entwined in the digital world: "[T]hose of us who live in the industrially developed parts of the Northern Hemisphere live and move and have our beings in the midst of our technologies" (*Technology and the Life-World* 2). Is "being in the midst" the kind of in-between that names the digital attitude? Terms that encapsulate the midst, like *medium*, as a middle or intermediate, center, and *media*, as an intermediary agency, figure prominently in these philosophical ideas. This intermediary place can be both collaborative and conflicting, a place where the user learns to *compromise*. The Latin prefix *com-* means to be with or together and the root of the word 'compromise' means to send forth or expect a future outcome or to assure that something will occur in a coming together that assures an outcome. The in-between, then, might be a coming together in the middle between other places or things or ideas.

In *The Mediatic Turn: Exploring Concepts for Media Pedagogy*, Norm Friesen and Theo Hug explain the in-between of digital media as a *mediatic* turn, an inter-penetration of every aspect of everyday activity in human-technology relations in cultural, epistemological, and existential terms. The mediatic turn emphasizes the in-between or the *mediator* in the digital media process as juxtaposed to everything in its totality in the lifeworld. In contrast, *mediatization* describes in Nick Couldry's "Mediatization or Mediation?" the converged social, cultural, and technological processes that create a format suitable for digital sharing. Another way of explaining the in-between is through the "generalized communicability of networks—a complete media environment in which mediation between humans and non-humans has retreated into the ambient background, leaving only *mediality*. In addition, the term *mediation* explains the results of flows of production, circulation, interpretation, and recirculation" (Couldry 383). Add to this the technological *mediation/mediation* theory, which further explores contemporary human-technology-world-relations (Ihde 1990, Rosenberger and Verbeek 2015). The I-technology-world schema moves through these relational shifts on a continuum that defines how the human and world connect through, in, and with technology.

TAKEN-FOR-GRANTED

Alfred Schütz and Thomas Luckmann explain the taken-for-granted in *The Structures of the Life-World* as a given in the lifeworld, the place where universal givens are part of everyday experience. In a world with many variables, the taken-for-granted is something we can count on as familiar because we have integrated life experiences, along with their successes and failures, into the vernacular of the everyday. The taken-for-granted is a habit of living that becomes "constituted in interpretations of experience (that is to say, explications of the horizon)" (9-10). Likewise, Maurice Merleau-Ponty explains the body's taken-for-granted movement in the lifeworld: "Visible and mobile, my body is a thing among things; it's caught in the fabric of the world, and its cohesion is that of a thing. But, because it moves itself and sees, it holds things in a circle around itself" (274). In "In Between Us: On the Transparency and Opacity of Technological Mediation," Yoni Van Den Eede frames the technological in between through transparency and opacity of technological mediation and recognizes the "double vision" in the process (157). For example, digital media largely occur and move, in/as form and content, through smart phones. Schütz explains, "In the natural attitude, I only become aware of the deficient tone of my stock of knowledge if a novel experience does not fit into what has up until now been taken as the taken-for-granted valid reference schema" (8). In contrast, Cathrine Hasse explains that from a cultural psychological perspective, the "meaning of socially constructed artifacts cannot be taken for granted" (53). She writes:

[A]ll artifacts are artificial . . . They are created by human beings—and their creation is never accidental, but embedded in human activity. Artifacts are created with purposes. They are tools meant to fulfil a desire or requirement developed in a cultural group of people, who pass not only material artifacts but also their cultural meaning on to the next generations through a process of learning. (48)

We thereby return to a question originally posed by Schütz and Luckmann: "What does it mean to take something for granted as simply given 'until further notice'?" (8) And how is that which has become questionable been transformed into something taken-for-granted? Is taken-for-grantedness something that we have learned through culturally embedded use? Has our digital media use been adopted as a given?

A SYMBIOTIC RELATIONSHIP

Digital media is symbiotic. The etymological notion of syn (together) and bios (live) seems a fitting naming of the human-technology relationship to digital media for the purposes of exploration. The digital media relationship is symbiotic. The form and content live together. As Marshall McLuhan argues in *Understanding Media*, the form of the medium embeds in the message. The characteristics of the medium are growing increasingly different by the minute while the medium/(digital) media are becoming more benign and more ubiquitous.

In gathering these ideas together, the digital attitude can be explored through blurred lines of the relationship between form and content of digital media in the Web 3.0 environment. The medium may be the message but the medium and the message are becoming even more ubiquitous and spreadable, taken-for-granted, overlapping, and co-shaped. We can make attitudinal choices about our technology but, at some level, we also need to recognize the fact that our attitudes are being formed by mere use and the collection of data that documents that use. Our personally conceived digital attitude is becoming less important because it can be derived from our use, not our opinion. Increasingly, data points of connection from digital movement within Web 3.0 along with data-mining for statistics on use, interest, and the proliferation of use, gives us more data than current technology can quickly make meaning of. . . at the moment. As noted in the introduction, all technologies come with the intended and unintended uses and contexts, both positive and negative, with planned and unplanned trajectories, transfers and multiplicities of use.

What is the digital attitude in a global environment where form and content blur? If our eyes are shut, will we even be paying attention? And do we still have a conscious *say* in cultivating and shaping the digital attitude of the future as communities, world citizens, philosophers, and educators? Are we seeing global, cultural, social, and political shifts based on digital media? Our logos is technology: it always places being in a relationship and assigns something to it. Our horizon is technology. Our intentionality is technology. Our perception is technology. The human-world has fully shifted to the "Human-technology-world" relationship (Ihde, *Technology and the Life-World* 85).

In contemporary society, more than ever before, life is mediated through digital media. The form, the content, and the *blur*, the in-between and the transformative—all need consideration. As Ihde explains in *Heidegger's Technologies: Postphenomenological Perspectives*, "there are many *varieties of technological experience*—one size does not fit all, and one analysis for all is next to useless" (120). Exploring the digital attitude is a pivotal step in the process. It seems possible, even likely, that the digital attitude of the future will be a co-shaping of humans and technologies. In *Postphenomenology and Technoscience: The Peking University Lectures,* Ihde also explains that, "This style of ontology carries with it a number of implications, including the one that there is a coconstitution of humans and their technologies" (44). Humans will need to figure out how much of a role to play in the digital attitude being formed.

So, how might the digital attitude be considered as we meet the edge of Web 3.0? As explained in the beginning of this reflection, our technologies and our digital media transform our experiences, perceptions, and interpretations of the world and this changes us in non-neutral ways. When technology seems take-for-granted or in-between or a given, its ubiquity still has a non-neutral and transformative impact on the world just by being there and being available for use. And perhaps, they become embedded in our cultural and social structures and in our learned behaviors. Where will this co-constituted, taken-for-granted and transformative, in-between and non-neutral shift move us as we consider the digital attitude in our increasingly technological era?

Works Cited

Couldry, Nick. "Mediatization or Mediation? Alternative Understandings of the Emergent Space of Digital Storytelling." *New Media and Society,* vol. 10, no. 3, 2008, pp. 373-391.

Friesen, Norm and Theo Hug. "The Mediatic Turn: Exploring Concepts in Media Pedagogy." *Mediatization: Concept, Changes, Consequences,* edited by Knut Lundby, Peter Lang Inc., International Academic Publishers, 2009.

Hasse, Cathrine. "Postphenomenology: Learning Cultural Perception in Science." *Human Studies,* vol. 31, no. 1, 2008, pp. 43-61.

Ihde, Don. *Heidegger's Technologies: Postphenomenological Perspectives.* Fordham University Press, 2010.

Ihde, Don. *Postphenomenology and Technoscience: The Peking University Lectures.* SUNY Press, 2009.

Ihde, Don. *Technology and the Life-World: From Garden to Earth.* Indiana University Press. 1990.

Jenkins, Henry, Joshua Green, and Sam Ford Jenkins. *Spreadable Media: Creating Value and Meaning in a Networked Culture.* New York University Press, 2013.

Manovich, Lev. *The Language of New Media.* The MIT Press, 2005.

McLuhan, Marshall. *Understanding Media: A McLuhan Sampler.* Toronto Education Quarterly, 1964.

Merleau-Ponty, Maurice. *The Visible and the Invisible.* Northwestern University Press, 1969.

Millard, David E., and Martin Ross. "Web 2.0: Hypertext by Any Other Name?" *HYPERTEXT '06: Proceedings of the Seventeenth Conference on Hypertext and Hypermedia,* 22-25 August 2006, pp. 27-30. *ACM Digital Library,* doi: 10.1145/1149941.1149947.

Rosenberger, Robert, and Peter-Paul Verbeek. *Postphenomenological Investigations: Essays on Human-Technology Relations.* Lexington Books, 2015.

Schütz, Alfred, and Thomas Luckmann. *The Structures of the Life-World*. Northwestern University Press, 1973.

Van Den Eede, Yoni. "In Between Us: On the Transparency and Opacity of Technological Mediation." *Foundations of Science*, vol. 16, no. 2-3, 2011, pp. 139-59.

Alexa Does Not Care. Should You? Media Literacy in the Age of Digital Voice Assistants

OLGA KUDINA
UNIVERSITY OF TWENTE
ENSCHEDE, THE NETHERLANDS

ABSTRACT: *This article explores the ethical dimension of digital voice assistants from the angle of postphenomenology and the technological mediation approach, whereby technology plays a mediating role in the human-world relations. Digital voice assistants, such as Amazon Echo's Alexa or Google's Home, increasingly form an integral part of everyday life for many people. Powered by Artificial Intelligence and based on voice interaction, voice assistants promise constant accompaniment by answering any questions people might have and even managing the physical space of their homes. However, while accompanying daily lives of people, voice assistants also seamlessly redefine the way people talk, interact and perceive each other. In view of their intentionalities, such as interaction by voice, command-based model of communication and development of attachment, digital voice assistant mediate the norms of interaction beyond their immediate use, the way people perceive themselves, those around and form consequent normative expectations. The article argues that understanding how technologies, such as digital voice assistants, mediate our moral landscape forms an essential part of media literacy in the digital age.*

KEYWORDS: postphenomenology, technological mediation, ethics of technology, digital voice assistants

1. INTRODUCTION

Digital voice assistants (DVAs) increasingly permeate households across the globe through our phones and smart speakers. Defined as devices that "can understand voice queries from a user and give audio responses or take actions on the user's behalf" (Google 1), DVAs promise a friendly and efficient accompaniment of the daily tasks, while interacting in natural language. Particularly DVAs in the form of smart speakers (e.g., Amazon's Echo, Google's Home, Xiaomi's Mi AI) reframe the medium of digital interaction from screens and keyboards to voice as interface. Such a shift in the mode of digital communication deserves philosophical attention for while DVAs help to switch on the lights in the house and provide weather forecast, they also seamlessly redefine the way we talk, interact, and perceive each other.

According to market estimates, one in five U.S. adults owns a smart speaker (Kinsella and Mutchler 6), with a total of 100 million smart speaker units to be installed globally by the end of 2018 (Kinsella par. 1). While official statistics report DVA proliferation among adults, it is children, particularly the preschoolers, who are frequent unintended DVAs users. Seduced by curt voice-based interaction that does not require reading and writing, children embrace DVAs that can continuously and patiently repeat things and answer their never-ending questions. However, children also mirror the way their parents interact with DVAs, which can be brisk, bossy, and harassing. As a result, some note the lack of manners children exhibit not only when interacting with Siri or Alexa, but also with their friends outside of home (Gonzalez).

As the global spread of DVAs increases, I would like to inquire about the ethical dimension of their use, particularly the co-shaping effect they have on the moral landscape of people. I will rely on the technological mediation approach Peter-Paul Verbeek advances for the field of postphenomenology in *What Things Do*. This theoretical prism allows to show how technologies mediate the way people relate to each other and to the world around by specific intentionalities they have. After I introduce DVAs and the theoretical background in more detail, I will review and reflect upon the current DVAs use practices through the lens of the technological mediation approach. I will conclude by suggesting an expansion of the global media literacy, namely that it should consider and account for the ethical dimension of technologies in the digital age.

2. Technological Mediation Approach

Don Ihde in *Technology and the Lifeworld* emphasizes the active role technologies play in how people perceive each other and how the world reveals itself to them. Consider how the mode of expression changes the experience of the narrator. Writing with a pen allows one to work at a slow pace, but also offers more opportunities to pause, carefully formulate the phrasing, and to observe the spelling norms. The word processor allows one to write much faster than when using a pen, which may give more room for creativity but also less room to think what one writes about. It also allows one to practically disregard the written aspects of language, delegating observation of writing norms to the pre-installed automatic spelling and grammar correction software, thus simultaneously expanding and silencing the cognitive experiences of the author. Dictating a story into one's digital device allows the narrator to follow the train of thoughts without interruptions for a keyboard or screen. Besides, the speed of producing material increases, given that people speak at 150 words per minute and type only 40 words in the same time (Watier sl. 7). While this can enhance self-expression, it can simultaneously reduce it by re-introducing the cumbersome task of editing the automatically transcribed text, often not perfect. These examples illustrate what Ihde calls *the intentionality of technology*, in this case for self-expression, whereby a pen, a word processor, and a voice-based interface each direct toward a specific use practice (48-49). Technological intentionality, put simply, refers to specific use practices that a technological design promotes, while making other use trajectories less visible, and as such suggests that technology is not neutral.

Ihde further explains the non-neutrality of technology when considering *technologies as mediators* of human experiences (16). When in use, technologies co-shape perceptions and actions of people, and as such, mediate the way people relate to each other and the world around them. Verbeek in *Toward a Theory of Technological Mediation* clarified the goals and scope of the technological mediation approach, originating in postphenomenology. Namely, the mediation approach explores the way technologies mediate the production of knowledge, ethical values, and metaphysical frameworks within specific human-technology-world relations. For this article, the ethical dimension of technological mediation is of particular interest, for it suggests that technologies co-shape moral frameworks by means of which people approach each other and these same technologies (Kudina and Verbeek 3).

As Verbeek argued in *Moralizing Technology*, if technologies help to shape the perceptions and actions of people, then the ethical consequence of this is that by framing human experiences in a certain way, technologies also co-shape the moral deliberations and decisions of people. The paradigmatic example of technological mediation of morality is the ultrasound, whereby by presenting a fetus in a specific way on the screen, ultrasound mediates parental decisions about abortion (ibid.) The technological mediation approach can help study how technologies constitute specific situations of choice and action, and as such mediate moral values or moralize the behavior of people. It can do so by studying specific human practices and experiences with a technology in question, drawing on pragmatism as one of the constituent influences on postphenomenology. In what follows, I will explore the ethical dimension of DVA uses with a view to the technological mediation of morality, as elaborated above.

3. UNDERSTANDING TECHNOLOGICAL INTENTIONALITIES OF DVAs

DVAs are a combination of software (AI-based voice assistant with the supporting cloud infrastructure) and hardware (the speaker, e.g. Amazon's Echo or Google's Home) that use voice as a primary interface. The way they operate is by reacting to a preset wake-word (e.g. "Alexa" or "Hey Google"), after which DVAs record the voice of the user, transmit it to the cloud-based services, and rely on natural language processing algorithms to interpret the speech of the user into appropriate commands. The commands can be local, such as asking DVA to tell a joke or to play music from its speakers; or they can apply to other devices in one's home, such as asking DVA to make coffee or to heat water in a bathtub, provided these devices are connected to the Internet and have a service subscription with that particular brand of DVA. One can also connect DVA to other businesses, such as taxi pick-up or pizza delivery, to request them to one's home. In short, DVAs promise to accompany the daily life of people, while being "helpful, informative, companionable, entertaining" (Vlahos par. 9).

From this description, one can deduce the primary technological intentionality of DVAs, namely to *interact via natural language*. Postphenomenologically speaking, this invites a perception of human-like communication and an expectation of DVAs as a conversation partner that understands you. However, conversational AI is still developing and is not perfect at speech recognition. Human conversations depend on the shared assumed meanings of a word or a phrase. For DVAs, grasping the intended meaning of jokes, words with double meanings or idiomatic expressions is still difficult. When users recognize that DVAs are no match for human interpretation, they frequently react with anger and frustration. But even foul language evokes friendly responses from DVAs, typically with phrases like "Well, thanks for the feedback!" and "That's nice of you to say!" even to openly offensive statements.

While short simplified interactions with DVAs can be irritating to some, they can be more profound to others. For example, DVAs help some adults and children to develop communication skills, transferrable to real life. DVAs can instill a question-answer based short and simple model of interaction, which can be helpful to people who struggle with communication. A mother of a child on the autism spectrum acknowledged a positive effect of her son frequently interacting with Apple's Siri:

My son's practice conversation with Siri is translating into more facility with actual humans. Yesterday I had the longest conversation with him that I've ever had. Admittedly, it was about different species of turtles […]. This might not have been my choice of topic, but it was back and forth, and it followed a logical trajectory. I can promise you that for most of my beautiful son's 13 years of existence, that has not been the case. (Newman par. 18)

The fact that DVAs offer friendly companionship at any time, are patient, and can repeat things to satisfy anyone's curiosity can explain such a beneficial spillover effect. However, apart from a positive therapeutic effect of DVAs, this example also demonstrates how interaction patterns with these technologies spread to the outside world, beyond immediate DVA use.

When people recognize the often-inapt responses of DVAs, as well as their soft respectful responses to any sort of query, they can try to test the limits of these devices. As Fessler notes, "Even if we're joking, [there is] the instinct to harass our bots" (par. 16). Fessler conducted a study of how different DVAs respond to direct sexualized insults, which appears to be a popular style of interaction with DVAs. According to the study, most of the DVAs provide neutral or flirtatious responses, such as "I'd blush if I could" or "How can you tell?" Bestowing female voices onto the majority of DVAs currently on the market helps Fessler argue that DVAs invite sexist perceptions of women, especially in their subservient role, and entrench existing gender stereotypes.

Viewed from a different angle, soft, patient responses encourage people to continuously turn to DVAs without fear of being judged. For instance, DVAs help dyslexic people to spell out the words. In personal communication, one of such users told me how DVA helps him to be a better version of himself and perform well in the academic job, relying much less on the help of other people. In this case, DVA becomes embodied as an extended part of the self through which the user realizes himself in the world. Such individual cases are essential to understand that while the soft, patient DVA responses invite impolite behaviors in some, for others they foster an open communication without worries about judgement and stigmatization.

Another technological intentionality concerns the ability of DVAs to *process speech as commands*. A user soon recognizes that speaking toward DVAs in the way we normally speak to people—with introductory words, politely, at times jokingly, using metaphors—only complicates the task-oriented DVAs in processing the user's language. Consequently, the habitual interaction with DVAs becomes curt, functional, and to the point. Such a command-based interaction can prompt a perception of a master-slave relationship, when "We want our technology to help us, but we want to be the bosses of it" (Hempel par. 9).

As the earlier example of DVAs helping to foster communication skills illustrated, the co-shaping relation between people, their devices, and the environment does not stop with the immediate technological interaction. It also does not stop at the door of morality (Swierstra 203). With the proliferation of DVAs, some adults noticed troubling children's behavior, such as exhibiting a lack of manners or being aggressive in interaction with peers (Gonzalez par. 1). As one of the parents noted, "I started saying 'please' occasionally after our three-year-old started barking orders at the speaker. Def[initely] changed our tone when making requests" (Lcg9q3 com. 14). As developmental psychologists Meltzoff and Prinz explain in *The Imitative Mind*, children learn social skills, get awareness of themselves and the others in mirroring the adults. While adults can distinguish between interaction patterns in different contexts, children have less experience in communication than the adults and rely on them as examples for learning social skills. American Academy of Pediatrics in their guidelines on *Media and Young Minds* suggest that children require active involvement of parents in setting desirable behavioral models and interaction norms when using digital technology. This insight is particularly relevant for the use of DVAs that already at the early stage of introduction demonstrate formative influence for the norms of communication and social courtesy.

Finally, as I will show below, *developing attachment* to DVAs also belongs to their technological intentionality, fostered by friendly (often female) voices, patient communication, and soft vocabulary. Liberati explained that people currently develop intimate relations with the "digital others," despite knowing that they are interacting with digital objects. Already in 1966, Weizenbaum, who developed the world's first autonomous conversational program ELIZA, found that people can develop close bonds with the program, even though all it did was providing an illusion of conversation by reshuffling parts of the user's sentences. Weizenbaum did not foresee a strong affection towards ELIZA, later realizing that even "extremely short exposures to a relatively simple computer program could induce powerful delusional thinking in quite normal people" (7).

Weizenbaum's discovery became known as the ELIZA effect, according to which even though people know that they face an artificial program/object, they treat it as if it were a real person who cares for them and behaves like them (Hofstadter ch. 4). It comes as no surprise that DVAs, with their carefully crafted personalities, naturally-sounding voices, and witty answers to the most mundane questions, intensify the ELIZA effect and can foster strong emotional bonds with their users.

Both adults and children alike come to rely on the friendly companionship DVAs provide. Alexa's presence provides comfort for adult users in different contexts, from making them feel less alone at home to restoring a feeling of companionship after the death of a partner (Calvin par. 25, 32-33). While adults consciously develop bonds with technologies, trying to overcome loneliness or looking for companionship, children might do so unwittingly. Returning to Newman's example with her son, Gus, she notes how he would bring his iPod along whenever they would go to the city, because he wanted the iPod to see his friends in the shop and not to feel lonely. One night, Newman (par. 25) witnessed a following conversation of Gus with Siri:

> Gus: Siri, will you marry me?
> Siri: I'm not the marrying kind.
> Gus: I mean, not now. I'm a kid. I mean when I'm grown up.
> Siri: My end user agreement does not include marriage.
> Gus: Oh, O.K.

This example shows how emotional bonds and affection that DVAs promote further blur the line in human-technology interaction in the age of DVAs. Moreover, DVAs provoke us to consider whether the fact that DVAs are not human makes a difference for the meaning of intimacy, friendship, trust, and other relations, traditionally associated with human beings and if so, to what extent.

4. Concluding Remarks: Moralizing Alexa and Siri

Reviewing different intentionalities of DVAs demonstrated how seemingly straightforward and useful technological features carry ethical implications. The advent of voice-first interfaces promises interaction in natural language, which fosters expectations of understanding interlocutors and helpful assistants. But while technologies are not yet a match for human interpretation, unfulfilled expectations may result in the perception of a master-slave relationship, with a human user bossing the world around via DVAs. This has implications for the morality of a conversation, whereby the top-down command-based interaction becomes a norm that surreptitiously seeps into the models of communication beyond DVAs. Moreover, the way people communicate undergoes a shift towards more functionality without seemingly unnecessary politeness or reciprocity. It is unlikely that such communication patterns will become the default reference for communication, for people can generally distinguish between the contexts and appropriate communication modes. However, as such DVA-promoted interaction patterns become more common, it might become more difficult to discern at what point they will penetrate our everyday language and the appropriate way of communication since what "appropriate communication" means might evolve together with these technologies.

Unlike adults, children have less reflective capacity to distinguish between different interaction contexts and may fall back, as they already do, on how their parents interact with DVAs at home. Because their experiential reference points are not yet rich, the earlier they learn what their parents might deem as undesirable communication norms, the more difficult it can be to correct them. DVAs thus provide a new dimension to an existing parental responsibility to lead by example.

The term "moralizing" in the heading of this section has a multistable meaning: it can be read both as referring to the moral mediation of DVAs by co-shaping our ethical behaviors and norms, and as a call to moralize the devices themselves both by using and designing them with the ethical implications in mind. In practice, it might mean saying "Thank you" to Alexa when Alexa does not care: it is the user herself toward whom this intentional politeness is directed. Considering being polite to DVAs, Gartenberg noted (par. 4):

As various people have made the argument to me, would you say "please" to a toaster or "thank you" to an ATM? But here's the thing. I don't talk aloud to an ATM or toaster. And I do when I'm asking Siri to turn on the lights or set an alarm, in the same natural language that I use in day-to-day life. It doesn't matter that an Echo can't hear or understand it — it matters that you say it.

Following the technological mediation approach, neither people nor technologies exist in a vacuum, but are co-dependent in shaping each other's environment, including the moral landscape. Reflecting on the use of DVAs, Turkle notes, "You yell at Alexa… you know Alexa is a machine. We treat machines as though they were people. And then, we are drawn into treating people as though they were machines" (qtd. in Fiegerman par. 11). Understanding how technologies mediate our relations between each other and with the world around is an essential form of media literacy in the digital age. The same way that DVAs help to develop human-human interactions, they also transform them in a less obvious way that often flies under the radar of designers and users alike. However, as I have tried to show in this article, the fact that the ethical dimension of technologies is less obvious does not make it less significant.

ACKNOWLEDGMENTS

This work was supported by the Netherlands Organization for Scientific Research (NWO) under a research program "Theorizing Technological Mediation: Toward an Empirical-Philosophical Theory of Technology," project number 277-20-006.

WORKS CITED

American Academy of Pediatrics. "Media and Young Minds." *Pediatrics*, 2016, vol. 138, no. 5, doi:10.1542/peds.2016-2591.Calvin, Aaron. "Can Amazon's Alexa be Your Friend?" *Digg*, 30 Mar. 2017, digg.com/2017/amazon-alexa-is-not-your-friend. Accessed 19 Dec.

2018.

Fessler, Leah. "Siri, Define Patriarchy." *Quartz*, 22 Feb. 2017, tiny.cc/1dimxy. Accessed 29 Aug. 2018.

Fiegerman, Seth. "Alexa, Shut Up: Raging Against the New Machines." *CNN*, 22 Aug. 2017, money.cnn.com/2017/08/22/technology/culture/personal-voice-assistants-anger/index.html. Accessed 28 Aug. 2018.

Gartenberg, Chaim. "Should You Say 'Please' and 'Thank You' to Your Amazon Echo or Google Home?" *The Verge*, 10 Dec. 2017, www.theverge.com/circuitbreaker/2017/12/10/16751232/smart-assistants-please-thank-you-politeness-manners-alexa-siri-google-cortana. Accessed Aug. 28, 2018.

Gonzalez, Robbie. "Hey Alexa, What Are You Doing to My Kid's Brain?" *Wired*, 5 Nov. 2018, www.wired.com/story/hey-alexa-what-are-you-doing-to-my-kids-brain/. Accessed 19 Dec. 2018.

Google. "Evaluation of Search Speech – Guidelines." *Google*, 13 Dec. 2017, storage.googleapis.com/guidelines-eyesfree/evaluation_of_search_speech_guidelines_v1.0.pdf. Accessed 29 Aug. 2018.

Hempel, Jessi, "Siri and Cortana Sound like Ladies Because of Sexism." *Wired*, 28 Oct. 2015, www.wired.com/2015/10/why-siri-cortana-voice-interfaces-sound-female-sexism/. Accessed Aug. 29, 2018.

Hofstadter, Douglas. *Fluid Concepts and Creative Analogies*. 1995, Basic Books.

Ihde, Don. *Technology and the Lifeworld: From Garden to Earth*. Indiana University Press, 1990.

Kinsella, Bret and Ava Mutchler. "Smart Speaker Consumer Adoption Report." *Voicebot.ai*, Mar. 2018, voicebot.ai/download-smart-speaker-consumer-adoption-report-2018/. Accessed 29 Aug. 2018.

Kinsella, Bret. "Smart Speakers to Reach 100 Million Installed Base Worldwide in 2018." *Voicebot.ai*, 10 July 2018, voicebot.ai/2018/07/10/smart-speakers-to-reach-100-million-installed-base-worldwide-in-2018-google-to-catch-amazon-by-2022/. Accessed 29 Aug. 2018.

Kudina, Olya, and Peter-Paul Verbeek. "Ethics from Within: Google Glass, the Collingridge Dilemma, and the Mediated Value of Privacy." *Science, Technology, & Human Values*, 1-24, doi:10.1177/0162243918793711.

Lcg9q3. Comment on "Should You Say 'Please' and 'Thank You' to Your Amazon Echo or Google Home?" *The Verge*, 10 Dec. 2017, 2:20 p.m., www.theverge.com/circuitbreaker/2017/12/10/16751232/smart-assistants-please-thank-you-politeness-manners-alexa-siri-google-cortana. Accessed Aug. 28, 2018.

Liberati, Nicola. "Facing the Digital Partner: A Phenomenological Analysis of Digital Otherness." *Glimpse*, vol. 19, 2018, pp. 99-107.

Meltzoff, Andrew N., and Wolfgang Prinz, editors. *The Imitative Mind. Development, Evolution, and Brain Bases*. Cambridge University Press, 2002.

Newman, Judith. "To Siri, with Love: How One Boy with Autism

Became BFF with Apple's Siri." *New York Times*, 17 Oct. 2014, www.nytimes.com/2014/10/19/fashion/how-apples-siri-became-one-autistic-boys-bff.html. Accessed 29 Aug. 2018.

Swierstra, Tsjalling. "Nanotechnology and Technomoral Change." *Ethica & Politica/Ethics & Politics*, 2013, vol. 15, no. 1, pp. 200-219.

Verbeek, Peter-Paul. *Moralizing Technology: Understanding and Designing the Morality of Things*. University of Chicago Press, 2011.

---. "Toward a Theory of Technological Mediation." *Technoscience and Post-phenomenology: The Manhattan Papers*, edited by Jan Kyrre Berg O. Friis and Robert P. Crease, Lexington Books, 2015, pp. 189-204.

---. *What Things Do: Philosophical Reflections on Technology, Agency, and Design*. Penn State Press, 2005.

Vlahos, James. "Inside the Alexa Prize." *Wired*, 27 Feb. 2018, www.wired.com/story/inside-amazon-alexa-prize/. Accessed 23 Aug. 2018.

Watier, Katherine. "SEO for Voice Search." SlideShare, 2 Dec. 2016, www.slideshare.net/katherinewatier/seo-for-voice-search. Accessed 28 Aug. 2018.

Weizenbaum, Joseph. *Computer Power and Human Reason: From Judgment to Calculation*. W. H. Freeman and Company, 1976.

Notes on Media Literacy and Illiteracy

PAUL MAJKUT

NATIONAL UNIVERSITY
LA JOLLA, CALIFORNIA, USA

ABSTRACT: *As an uncritical theoretical presupposition, the notion of literacy has led to formalistic, bookish philosophy. The constipated philosophical discourse adjudged worthwhile by literati and digirati falls historically into a line of dogmatic argument and counterargument within academic tradition submerged in subjective-idealist solipsism, petit-bourgeois political apologetics, and economic escapism. Careerist generalization of literacy from the ability to read print to include metaphoric uses of the term "literacy" to all media, while comfortably foggy to irrationalists, adds little to our understanding of print or other media except by increasing the gloom that prevails among privileged, neo-liberal pettifoggers.*

KEYWORDS: bookish philosophy, digital literacy and illiteracy, *le langue vécu*, copying and creativity, the primacy or orality

As an uncritical theoretical presupposition, the notion of literacy has led to formalistic, bookish philosophy. The constipated philosophical discourse adjudged worthwhile by literati and digirati falls historically into a line of dogmatic argument and counterargument within academic tradition submerged in subjective-idealist solipsism, petit-bourgeois political apologetics, and economic escapism. Careerist generalization of literacy from the ability to read print to include metaphoric uses of the term "literacy" to all media, while comfortably foggy to irrationalists, adds little to our understanding of print or other media except by increasing the gloom that prevails among privileged, neo-liberal pettifoggers.

Practitioners within the literary history of ideas whose self-interest apparently provides intellectual foundation enough for their thought, include *literacy* as a cornerstone of civilization. By fiat, to be civilized is to be able to read and write, illiteracy is deemed *barbaric,* and the tyranny of the literate wordsmith is further empowered by written representation. While these elitist judgments are thought of as cultural, they are at root economic.

Assumed uncritically, "language" is offered as the "house of Being," and codified philosophic-academic writing, often esoteric and obscure, is its fastidious housekeeper. While this would be a pretty big house if language were a castle, a house is not a home. Fortunately, within the less flamboyant context of media studies, it is the *book itself* (codex, scroll, manuscript, print, electronic, etc.) that is more appropriately thought of as the *house of Being.* Perhaps "suburb of Being" is a better metaphor. Academic enterprise is, after all, an endless housing development of any number of mediated texts (books), some shabby dwellings, some condominiums, some palaces that contain many empty rooms, but more often coffins in library cemeteries.

Just as "literacy" has been vaporized into semantic smoke, so too have the terms "book," "text," and "read" been deluded to the extent that they have lost their diachronic roots. It follows, then, that in discussing "media literacy," we must take care to avoid slipping on ever-shifting meanings clouded in metaphor and uncritical usage.[1]

Within the antipodes of *literacy* and *illiteracy*, greater literacy is assumed as an indication of intelligence. The ability of a society to weigh its own words by recording its own history as an external, stored memory is, it is claimed, the measure of all things civilized. The exercise of this ability by intellectuals is problematic, not because we question the agency of the exercise, but because the character masks of academic agents must be removed in order to see them face-to-face. Once we remove the fraudulent notion that "intelligence" is genetic and, therefore, hereditary ("Cyril Burt"), once we discard the subjective idealist cornerstone, the individual, and see that intelligence is purely social, the agent becomes clearly seen as a worker who primarily uses his mind, not his hands, to do his work. As such, we see the agent as someone who works within an intelligentsia and whose ideas are formed by the relationships found within that group. It should not be thought that the distinction made between mind and manual labor is absolute, for all labor involves a skill of one kind or another. In this understanding, there is no such thing as "unskilled labor," another pretention and self-serving distinction originated by the bourgeoisie and implemented by their petty-bourgeois servants in order to justify exploitative pay. Of course, this is an intricate ideology in which the individual philosopher sees himself in terms of Platonic philosopher-kings, Nietzschean *Übermensch*, and literate-intellectual Ayatollahs.

Although there is a marked difference in an individual's passive reading and active spoken vocabulary, the number of words recognized in passive (above all, *silent*) reading and active, spoken vocabulary, cannot be used to gauge greater awareness. Speed reading, for instance, allows a reader to reach a goal sooner (the end of a lineated text) but does not assure the reader that he understands where he is going or the significance of the end reached. An ending, after all, need not be a conclusion. All conclusions are endings, but all endings are not conclusions. Vocabulary, a social system, is never individual and what some have posited as "idiolects" are in various forms and various degrees signs of solipsistic linguistic disfunction. Idiolects are consciously established by listeners when they enter social discourse, not speakers who unconsciously enter a non-communicative realm of discourse.

History is the consequence of literacy, it is maintained, and thinkers

---

[1] The reader will forgive my use of tropes in this discussion, but metonymy, synecdoche, simile, and metaphor are a refuge of the near hopeless, and, after all, any number of modern and post-modern philosophers are given to metaphor—usually bad metaphors that cannot be extended or, in the spirit of 17th-century, "metaphysical conceits" mixed in an unruly fashion.

such as Vilém Flusser add that since history is written as a text within a concrete medium, the book, it is linear representation. He fails to distinguish between straight-linearity and curvi-linearity. The linearity of text in book media is imposed by its structure. All media, including some forms of the book, however, are not straight-linear. Flusser's narrow identification of writing as a Greek historical phenomenon ignores non-linear media. I have elsewhere called attention to this difference:

> The existence of linearity in pre-alphabetic and pre-syllabic inscriptions, neglected by Flusser and others, is perhaps overlooked not because it lacks straight-linearity but takes other linear forms ... at times, the spiral, curved linearity found on the two-sided Minoan Phaistos Disc, which, it is generally agreed, is read from the center out. (Majkut 87).

The Phaistos Disc is an historical, written, curvilinear document—not a "prehistoric" document—so it must fall within Flusser's identification of history with writing. Herbert Brekle notes that:

> An early clear incidence for the realization of the typographic principle is the notorious Phaistos Disc (ca. 1800–1600 BC). If the disc is, as assumed, a textual representation, we are really dealing with a "printed" text, which fulfills all definitional criteria of the typographic principle. The spiral sequencing of the graphemic units, the fact that they are impressed on a clay disc (a process known as "blind printing") and not imprinted, is merely a possible technological variant of textual represent-ation. The decisive factor is that the material 'types' are proven to be repeatedly instantiated on the clay disc. (58)

The point made here is that the Phaistos Disc is an extant typographical artifact that employed moveable print impressed on clay, not printed on paper, and was spiral, curve-linear, not straight-linear. This means that Flusser's metaphorical "line" of history is not always straight and that at least two forms of historic narrative are possible.

THE PHAISTOS DISC, SIDE A, AND DETAIL (BELOW). "PHAISTOS DISK." WIKIPEDIA, HTTPS://COMMONS.WIKIMEDIA.ORG/WIKI/CATEGORY:PHAISTOS_DISK. ACCCESSED 29 JUNE

Cyclical history is recurrent history, *saecula*, externally stored "memory" that is experienced generationally, a record of living history marked by externalized generational memory. In this sense, history "repeats itself" because the curvilinear medium is closely aligned to recurrent patterns of nature. Historical memory is measured time. Mediated, cyclical history repeats itself in variations of natural themes—astronomical events, the earth's seasons, life and death.

Language captured visually is partially captured. *Le langue vécu*,[2] unlike its mediated representation, is governed by linguistic change at all levels (phonetically, lexically, syntactically, semantically), but, when transformed into "texts," visually or in recorded speech, it is mediated and, therefore, representational. We caution ourselves not to fall into the commonplace mistake of equating living, spoken, spontaneous language (de Saussure's *la parole*) with recorded sound, which is no less representational than the printed word in a book or an image. Further, we should not allow the easy acceptance of "simultaneous" communication in digital media as communication that is not mediated. Two-way, digital synchronicity is representational—not unmediated communication. On the contrary, mediated texts in any medium are dead texts incapable of growth, therefore incapable of dialectic movement. The date, for example, on the colophon page (backside of the title page) in a printed book, is a tombstone noting the time of death of *le langue vécu*, the moment when the living body of language became a mediated corpse.

Here we look not only to the technological nature of media, their structures and functions, but also survey the economic ground from which media grow and political actions create ethical value. The saying, *politics is ethics writ large*, is the sky that overhangs our discussion. Ultimately, as we are freed of our mediated chains, the mediated reading and writing processes that underpin our understanding, we return not only to the reign of orality, but also the world of political action, recognizing ourselves as species being, removing our ideological character masks, and finding ourselves to be *zoon politikon*—living political animals—who grasp that "philosophers have only interpreted the world" as Marx wrote famously. Removing ourselves from mediation places us once again in a natural world of the deed, of action, and this freedom allows us to become activists. Political animals are by nature activists and it is impossible to think of the political animal as anything other than a political activist.

Questions of literacy, its meaning and socio-economic use, imply questions of illiteracy without stating them. Often, an incomplete meaning of literacy is assumed uncritically. One such bookish assumption, accepted without reflection, is that illiteracy is the *lack* of literacy, that is the inability to read. It is simply not the case that illiteracy *follows literacy as a consequence* either cognitively or historically.

The concept of literacy is also incomplete unless its definition

---

[2] I have coined the term *le langue vécu* for Saussure's *la parole* to parallel Merleau-Ponty's *le corps vécu*.

includes writing as the other leg upon which it walks—and, even with that inclusion, it walks backwards: *preliterate* orality precedes literacy. But it is not the ability to read and write that defines humanity but spoken language. Were our beloved prehistoric paleolithic and neolithic ancestors human? History is only possible with literacy, and literacy is always susceptible to the defacements inherent in any material medium. If we grant that our preliterate grandmothers and grandfathers were capable of empathy, then we accept that they had conscience, ethics, politics, and wisdom.

Reading and writing are two aspects of the same representational code: *literacy*. Originally meaning "educated, learned, one who knows the alphabetic letters" (Latin *literatus/literatus*), the ability to read an alphabetic text. More concretely, this ability referred to an understanding of manuscript scripts and, eventually, fonts in print. Whether handmade or machine-made was not a consideration, although late scriptoria apologists in their arguments against print understood "writing" as *copying*, not intellectual *creativity*. Imaginative storytelling was distinct from writing, though today the term is used interchangeably for creative writing. The distinction between writing as copying and writing as an imaginary practice is common. Both "reading" and "literacy" are now understood in a broader sense to mean *understanding* or *interpreting* written or drawn symbols as well as auditory media. We *read*, for example, person's facial expression. We *read* digital representation, *read* a work of art, *read* the mood of a nation, and so forth. While this connotative sense of the term "read" has been inherent in English since Anglo-Saxon /ræd/, it is potentially misleading in Modern English. The sense of "read" has shifted radically since the invention and mass consumption of printed and now digital texts. The mass production of books, reducing their cost, means that more and more people buy them, which entailed the ability to read coded representation. No longer was a *Reader* a medieval scholar who stood at a lectern with one costly book delivering its content *orally* to students who wrote what they heard. University and monastic scriptoria could not keep up with the demand. The invention of print accompanied and was made a technological necessity by a growing mercantile class. With this, medieval public reading aloud became a private event and the role of the reader was shifted from the oral performance of a text to a visual, silent reading. The reader became one who read to himself, though the primacy of orality remained in place—consciously found in children's insistence to hear a text repeated by an adult reader, unconsciously in silent-reading subvocalization (auditory reassurance), the slight movement of vocal cords in the vocal tract. Subvocalization, however, is a disappearing link in silent reading that eventually leads to the severance of silent reading from language and, finally, to solipsism. The more one reads, the more one is detached from language. Subvocalization means, strictly, that a text in some sense always remains a performance script, that reading itself is always a performance, even though the performer and the audience are identical in silent reading. In this, we may say that the stages of literacy evolution discussed above are not solely historical or diachronic, but that all historical stages are still present at one and the same time.

In addition, the interiorization of reading that accompanies silent reading with the growth of printed materials removes the act of reading from the public sphere (to be *read to*) to the private sphere, breaking the auditory feed-back loop necessary to living, evolving spoken language and replacing it with static, dead text. Silent internalization of a read text is a private matter, depriving the reader of corrective feedback since he is at one time the reader and the read-to of what is read. This lack of linguistic corrective together with the static nature of mediated language inevitably leads to solipsistic expression in which the silent reader detaches himself from the world around him and, as a writer, speaks only to himself and is understood by himself. This phenomenon is no less true of digital media than it is of paper and other media.

The colophon date of publication is the tombstone for the textual body of decomposing etymological meaning, the book is its coffin, and reading a funeral ceremony attended by the solitary silent writer-reader.

Reading that is interiorized is subjectivized, made private, and becomes withdrawn from objective, public feedback. The private act of writing subsumed us by the act of reading, the author extolled, and text becomes "authoritative." Without the linguistic loop, year by year the text becomes more solipsistic, ultimately unintelligible to any but the author in a welter of neologisms and coined expressions, as found in much hermeneutic writing. The dying of language is set on an evolutionary path when the internalized writer-reader becomes silent.

The question is not only how media structures knowledge, in general, and philosophy, in particular, leading to "bookish philosophy," but also one of the dominance of "literacy" as the criterion of "superior" knowledge or understanding; therefore, we are troubled by failure of the literate to consider that their knowledge is mediated bookish philosophy. Non-literate (oral) is not "illiterate" in this inferior sense. The term *illiterate* is prejudicial when it defines the inability to read as a *lack*. But learning, of course, need not be mediated, not confined to literacy, and wisdom rarely is.

Let us think a little more about literacy as the ability to read encoded visual and phonic representation. In *Writing Systems: A Linguistic Introduction*, Geoffrey Sampson argues against the notion of those who maintain that writing is "a phenomenon essentially parasitic on spoken language" (29-30). Sampson misses the point. Although "parasitic" is a strong word, it accurately describes the dependent relationship of written representation of language and language itself. Sampson's rejection of the parasitic nature of written code is a tacit rejection of de Saussure's clear understanding that "language and writing are two distinct systems of signs: the second exists for the sole purpose of representing the first"— which is another way of saying that writing is a parasite on *le langue vécu* (23).

Learning has become bookish and wears textual meaning like a shroud. Literati insist on a hierarchy of values assigned to learning that ranges from literate down to illiterate, a bias favoring mediated learning, though in the world we see that learning comes primarily through doing. I have spoken of "bookish philosophy" or thinking geared to various protocols of mediated reading and writing and of how this results in *bookish philosophy*, but now we face the same problem in electronic media, "digital philosophy," and ask how digitalization informs and defaces knowledge. Just as there are limitations to bookish philosophy, we question the limitations and distortions of digital philosophy. We ask how and in what sense is the mobile literacy of a smartphone "smart"; we wonder if digital philosophy and the literacy required of its medium restricts thought by offering more choices, less variety; we question the uses of media literacy as democratic.

Obvious limitations are seen in the processes of writing and reading: cut-and-paste composition in writing that replaces linear, syllogistic reasoning with associative matrix reasoning, overwhelming intertextuality in embedded click-reading, and an intertextuality that dismisses or ignores textual autonomy.

Communicative mobility exaggerates economic immobility and, in its most unfettered practice, encourages the exploitative excesses of neoliberal capitalism, widens the gap between haves and have-nots, and, in the current assault on egalitarian distribution of wealth, solidifies unregulated anarcho-fascism unleashed by libertarian cryptocurrencies such as Bitcoin (DowneastDem). Unlike the craft labor of artisans in the Middle Ages, when life and work were integrated as cottage industry, labor is today alienated from its product and becomes its own commodity transformed by anti-social media disguised as "social" media.[3] We are confronted with California ideology ("Californian Ideology") and libertarian-fascist transhumanism ("Transhumanist Politics"), both resting on antiquated notions of media as though they could be lifted analytically from history and served up as a main course of aphoristic insights:

> With McLuhan as its patron saint, the Californian ideology has emerged from this unexpected collision of right-wing neo-liberalism, counter-culture radicalism and technological determinism—a hybrid ideology with all its ambiguities and contradictions intact. These contradictions are most pronounced in the opposing visions of the future which it holds simultaneously. (Barbrook and Cameron)

Resting on class-based educationalist ideology, "literacy" has long-served the vested interests of those with a specific skill in a world in which there are only skilled humans, privileging that narrow skill above all others and serving to justify class actions.

The dead have nothing to say to the living. The scratchings on this paper have not escaped the bookish philosophy and death that it reviles but should not be understood solely as signs of despair. They are not the medieval philosopher's fingernail

---

[3] "Unskilled" labor is, at best, neglected by Silicon Valley ideologs as though it did not exist; at worst, denigrated.

scratches on the lid of his coffin indicating despair, a sin that prohibited him from entering heaven. Yes, my scratchings are failed attempts to escape premature burial, but this coffin is not a lonely place. You, after all, are also here.

WORKS CITED

"Cyril Burt." *Wikipedia*, en.wikipedia.org/wiki/Cyril_Burt. Accessed 10 June 2019.

"The Californian Ideology." *Wikipedia*, 10 September 2018, en.wikipedia.org/wiki/The_Californian_Ideology. Accessed 10 June 2019.

"Transhumanist Politics." *Wikipedia*, 29 January 2019, en.wikipedia.org/wiki/Transhumanist_politics#Libertarian_transhumanism. Accessed 10 June 2019.

Barbrook, Richard, and Andy Cameron. "The Californian Ideology." *Mute,* vol. 1, no. 3, 1 September 1995, www.metamute.org/editorial/articles/californian-ideology. Accessed 10 June 2019.

Brekle, Herbert E. "Das typographische Prinzip. Versuch einer Begriffsklärung." *Gutenberg-Jahrbuch*, vol. 72, 1997, pp. 58–63.

DowneastDem. "Anarcho-Fascism: The Libertarian Endgame." *Daily Kos,* 15 June 2010, www.dailykos.com/stories/2010/6/15/876205/-. Accessed 10 June 2019.

Majkut, Paul. Smallest Mimes: Defaced Representation and Media Epistemology. Bucharest: Zeta Books, 2014.

Preston, Keith. "'Anarcho-Fascism': An Overview of Right-Wing Anarchist Thought." *Attack the System: Pan-Anarchism Against the State, Pan-Secessionism Against the Empire,* 20 November 2016, attackthesystem.com/2016/11/20/anarcho-fascism-an-overview-of-right-wing-anarchist-thought/. Accessed 10 June 2019.

Saussure, Ferdinand de. *Course in General Linguistics*, edited by Charles Bally and Albert Sechehaye in collaboration with Albert Reidlinger, translated by W. Baskin, Fontana 1974.

Sampson, Geoffrey. *Writing Systems: A Linguistic Introduction*. Stanford University Press, 1985.

Digital Dissent on WikiLeaks: Anonymous Whistleblowers in the Shadow of Julian Assange

RIANKA ROY

SURENDRANATH COLLEGE FOR WOMEN
CALCUTTA UNIVERSITY
KOLKATA, INDIA

ABSTRACT: *This paper is a review of WikiLeaks—a prominent name in digital dissent. It was founded by Julian Assange in 2006. Since its inception, the organization has been exposing classified state and corporate documents on its website to common users of the Internet. Anonymous whistleblowers provide WikiLeaks with content. It creates a new methodology of uniting digital media and journalism. It uses information in an unprecedented way to reveal state and corporate transgressions. This paper analyses how WikiLeaks contributes to information-based capitalism. While the site is a commendable venture to reveal state and corporate secrets, WikiLeaks is not free from its flaws. This paper critiques the way Assange robs whistleblowers of their identities and voices and presents himself as a surrogate hero.*

KEYWORDS: Julian Assange, WikiLeaks, whistleblowers, surveillance, journalism

1. INTRODUCTION

Founded in 2006, by 2010 WikiLeaks has become a prominent name in the field of digital activism in the wake of its major breakthroughs like Collateral Murder (video footage from the helicopter cockpit showing the killing of Iraqis); Afghan War Logs (classified documents on the Afghan War); the Iraq War Logs and Cablegate (US diplomatic cables on wars). Its leak of Hillary Clinton's emails provoked a major controversy before the US presidential polls in 2017. With its small team of reporters led by Julian Assange, the organization claims to be "a giant library of the world's most persecuted documents" (About, WikiLeaks).

WikiLeaks differs from the usual model of news reporting or even investigative journalism. It is not run by any capitalist corporation. It is built by and around Assange and exposes state and corporate secrets. Its counter-surveillance mechanism makes it "an alternative platform that encourages whistle-blowing to flourish" (Thorsen *et al* 102). In "The Nihilism of Julian Assange" published by *The New York Review of Books*, Sue Halpern points out that, "Assange's goal was to hold power—state power, corporate power, and powerful individuals—accountable by offering a secure and easy way to expose their secrets." The subversive stance of the website initially aligned it with leftist ideology. However, Donald Trump's use of Hillary Clinton's emails leaked on WikiLeaks proved the website to be a resource open to uses by any state, corporate, or individual entity (Smith).

Unlike social networking sites, WikiLeaks does not require its users to maintain a profile in order to leak information. While state and corporations run covert surveillance on citizens, WikiLeaks is transparent about its vigilance to expose state and corporate atrocities. It rigidly maintains the privacy and security of its contributors. Anonymous contributors send classified information to an electronically encrypted drop box, which, according to WikiLeaks, conceals whistleblowers' identities even from the website's editors. This protects whistleblowers from litigation.

This method has enabled Assange, the founder of WikiLeaks, to emerge as a representative of all whistleblowers. He faces censure from various countries and companies. His own struggle validates and contributes to narratives that testify to exploitation of citizens by the state and its agents. Assange represents the entire community of whistleblowers without uniting them and without being a whistleblower himself. This makes him a messianic figure: a vigilant warrior with an eschatological vision heralding the end of corruption. He seizes upon the collective memory of state atrocities and disrupts the cycle of conformism. To use Walter Benjamin's terms from "Theses on the Philosophy of History" (1940), Assange is a chronicler who is both the redeemer and the vanquisher of the Antichrist and who saves men from becoming tools in the hands of the ruling classes (247).

2. Identity and Method of WikiLeaks

The status of WikiLeaks remains a debatable issue. On the one hand, it is a new-generation representative of the fourth estate; on the other hand, it is acknowledged to be a subversion of the same. Yochai Benkler argues that networks of this kind are merely an altered form of traditional media, or the "networked fourth estate" (12). He even adds that mainstream news media deliberately "denigrate the journalistic identity" of WikiLeaks in order to protect their own status (12). However, there seems to be a difference between WikiLeaks and other news media in terms of content. WikiLeaks provides documents for the perusal of its global audience, often without redaction. It resembles more of an archive than a newspaper or a journal. Users contribute documents, and they themselves explore them. WikiLeaks seemingly follows the pattern of citizen journalism and upholds the participatory principle of Web 2.0. The near-absence of editorial intervention makes the content more open towards the audience than an edited news report/video. At the same time, it invites the audience, inclusive of journalists, to create stories from the raw material. Therefore, WikiLeaks is a mediator between whistleblowers and their audience.

Slavoj Žižek claims that there is no novelty in the content of WikiLeaks. It merely provides documentary evidence of corporate corruption and state totalitarianism. Its radical method of disclosure evokes controversy. Writing for the *London Review of Books* in 2011, Žižek reflects that, "[t]he aim of the WikiLeaks revelations was not just to embarrass those in power but to lead us to mobilize ourselves to bring about a different functioning of power that might reach beyond the limits of representative democracy" (9-10). He claims that WikiLeaks fulfils this aim by providing documentary evidence of state and corporate atrocities of which the citizens already have some vague idea or common knowledge. The very act and method of enunciation—i.e. providing evidence of obvious malpractices—challenges conventional modes of journalism and the usual channels of dialogue. It unsettles preexisting power relations. In an article published in *The Guardian* in 2014, Žižek also states that WikiLeaks "undermines the very principle of spying, the principle of secrecy, since its goal is to make secrets public." Digital tools provide Wiki-Leaks with the unique advantage of constructing alternative power structures based on information and surveillance.

The importance of its content, however, cannot be ignored. Documents on state and corporate malpractices expose well-guarded secrets. However, WikiLeaks also needs to construct a narrative to present the stories to the masses in comprehensible forms. Two factors have enabled WikiLeaks to make itself more relatable to the masses: its collaboration with five newspapers from five countries (*El País* from Spain, *Le Monde* from France, *Der Spiegel* from Germany, *The Guardian* from the United Kingdom, and *The New York Times* from the United States) that make the citizens aware of what WikiLeaks does, and the status of Assange as a hero persecuted for unmasking the state and its corporate allies.

3. WIKILEAKS, TRUTH AND THE CULT OF ASSANGE

Pramod Nayar refers to Michel Foucault's discourse on *parrhesia* while examining the role of WikiLeaks in society. In his lectures titled "Discourse and Truth: The Problematization of *Parrhesia*," Foucault traces the history of the word *parrhesia* from its Greek origin through its use by the Romans and shifts of meaning under Christianity. This act of enunciation, according to Foucault, indicates a relationship between the speaker and what he says. In free speech, the speaker makes it clear that what he says is entirely his opinion (3). The ideal *parrhesiastes* is courageous and speaks truth to power at the cost of his safety (3). Nayar adapts this theory to his analysis of how Assange runs WikiLeaks. He claims that the digital *agora* or the Internet is a compromised space: "the domain where democracy itself is at stake" (30). It is overpowered by conventional hegemonic bodies. States and corporations rather than citizens determine the scope of digital access. Digital surveillance on the networked public is no longer a matter of speculation. However, Nayar states that WikiLeaks exposes "the making of the world order (or disorder)" by resorting to *parrhesia*—the act of telling the truth—at a substantial risk, from a position of subordination, against authorities (28).

Perhaps Žižek is right to point out that there is nothing new in the content of WikiLeaks, as the latter gathers documentary evidence of corruption that people have common or vague knowledge of, but the site devises a new method of *parrhesia* in the networks. In this new form of *parrhesia*, the actual *parrhesiastes* is silent and anonymous. He is merely a messenger; his only function is to supply documents to WikiLeaks. Assange is a surrogate *parrhesiastes* speaking on behalf of anonymous whistleblowers, yet he emerges as the primary representative of truth, so that his identity becomes a brand. Nayar develops his argument on the basis of Foucault's theory of *parrhesia*, where the *parrhesiastes* claims to present his own opinion. What Assange presents to his audience is technically neither his opinion nor a result of his original research and investigation. Nayar does not explain if a proxy *parrhesiates* also deserves the same honor of the actual *parrhesiastes*. In a description of what the organization does, in an article titled 'What is WikiLeaks,' dated November 3, 2015, the site distances itself from states and corporations and claims to represent the "general public." However, Assange's identity overshadows actual whistleblowers as he appropriates their voices and enforces organizational principles on them. It becomes a counter-organization to states and corporations.

Assange faces persecution, and since 2012 he is confined to the Ecuadorian embassy in London. His eviction from the embassy may be imminent (Topping). However, he faces charges of rape, not of *parrhesia*. This is generally understood as the retaliation of the state against Assange. His role as the *parrhesiastes* and his appearance as the sole crusader made it impossible to determine if the retaliation was against him or against WikiLeaks. Companies like Master Card, Visa, PayPal, and Bank of America refused to carry out financial transactions for WikiLeaks in 2010 (Greenberg). Nayar argues that these attempts to vilify Assange overshadow his commitment to truth (29). I contend that, Assange uses this persecution to his advantage—since he emerges as the *parrhesiastes*, the sole crusader, a troubled hero.

Assange's isolation—as seen in his confinement at the Ecuadorian embassy in London—also fits well into the structure of isolation of digital network users. The Ecuadorian government granted him asylum in 2012, but recent reports about Assange facing the risk of eviction from the embassy are all too visible (Valencia). However, this further affirms his status as the *parrhesiates* who necessarily faces danger because of the act of telling truth. He is the icon of all users of the Internet, which has become an oppressive network in the hands of states and corporations running websites, and revolts from within that space. His voice—or ventriloquism since he speaks on behalf of others—overshadows all users who are already isolated on digital networks in digital capitalism.

Assange's stellar appearance on media promotes a personality cult with "media-moderated mass support" (Hutnyk). His towering presence makes up for the invisibility of whistleblowers and editors. In this identity-based hegemony, whistle-blowing is no longer an individualistic pursuit, an act of choice, and a performance of revelation. Rather, it becomes an anonymous act of supplying information to the site which presents the information as commodity to an audience in a palatable form. Even if in some cases redaction or editing is avoided, the selection of content remains the prerogative of WikiLeaks editors. According to the WikiLeaks submission guidelines, "WikiLeaks accepts *classified, censored* or otherwise *restricted* material of *political, diplomatic or ethical significance*. WikiLeaks *does not accept* rumour, opinion or other kinds of first hand reporting or material that is already publicly available."

WikiLeaks does not give contributors the choice to reveal their identities even if they wish to. In the noble—and patronizing—act of keeping its contributors anonymous and safe from prosecution, WikiLeaks robs whistleblowers of their due recognition. In the act of whistleblowing, it is certainly not necessary to reveal one's identity. However, Assange's assertion of his identity is founded upon the forced anonymity of whistleblowers. He takes the credit for assembling the information, while the actual whistleblowers have no choice to reveal their identities. It is disturbingly evident in the blog posts and articles published on WikiLeaks that Assange turns himself into a towering figure in the world of secrets without acknowledging the contribution of whistleblowers.

Anonymity is not a condition of whistleblowing, but for whistleblowers on WikiLeaks it is. The content of disclosures, too, avoids putting much emphasis on individuals. Even when disclosures target individual personalities, as, for example, in the release of Hillary Clinton's and John Podesta's emails, the persons represent a political party or a state. Such suppression of other individuals reinforces Assange's centrality in the world of networked individualism.

Edward Snowden chose a mainstream newspaper, *The Guardian,* for revealing the secrets of the National Security Agency surveillance program. As a result, he could reach out immediately to a large number of citizens. He disclosed his identity soon after the revelation (Elgot). By avoiding the WikiLeaks path, he spared himself the fate of oblivion and anonymity. His disclosure found due prominence without becoming yet another batch of files in WikiLeaks database.

The proclaimed concern of WikiLeaks for whistleblowers' safety is rather dubious. The site did nothing much to defend Chelsea Manning after he faced charges of treason for leaking war-related diplomatic cables to WikiLeaks. The organization tweeted that if Barack Obama granted Manning clemency, Assange would turn himself in. When Manning finally received clemency, Assange did not act on its words. Instead, he stated that the government tried to harass him with Manning's clemency (Hunt). In some ways, WikiLeaks tried to make the news more about Assange than Manning as always attributing the agency of disruption and the fate of agony to Assange.

The absolute control over technical resources of the site sustains Assange's aura as a heroic figure in the world of whistleblowing. Like mainstream social media, WikiLeaks, too, runs a structured and well-governed system, reminiscent of Foucauldian governmentality, by making contributors conform to its conditions. Whistleblowers have to follow the predetermined pattern of uploading content. The status of its contributors is to some extent similar to that of unpaid and exploited laborers (or common users) in digital social media. Contributors provide confidential information, and WikiLeaks capitalizes on information it publicizes on its site. The socio-political response it elicits reinforces its image as a brand. On the basis of this popularity, it seeks financial support for its projects in the form of donations and through the sale of merchandise.

WikiLeaks collaborates predominantly with five newspapers, *The Guardian*, *The New York Times*, *Der Spiegel*, *El País*, and *Le Monde* to publicize its acquisition of materials. The site insists that the mode of collaboration should keep WikiLeaks as the chief owner of information. Assange's occasional disagreements with various newspapers make it clear that the organization is not keen on relinquishing its control over information (Katz).

For instance, in July and October of 2010, without first posting the Afghan War Logs on its site, WikiLeaks shared them with *The New York Times*, *The Guardian*, and *Der Spiegel*. It was decided that the papers would not publish reports on the documents until WikiLeaks released the material to acknowledge WikiLeaks as the primary source of information. On July 25, the newspapers independently published their stories on the War Logs, on all 92000 documents. WikiLeaks, meanwhile, posted a database containing only 76,911 of the documents.

On November 28, 2010, WikiLeaks announced that it was in possession of 251,287 diplomatic cables pertaining to the Afghan War from the American State Department as well as from the United States embassies and consulates. The project was titled Cablegate. WikiLeaks released the cables in batches in coordination with various news organizations. *The New York Times* had refused to publish WikiLeaks's war logs databases earlier and, instead, criticized Assange. Hence, WikiLeaks did not share the cables with *The New York Times* and had asked *The Guardian* to do the same. However, since others had copies of the cables, *The Guardian* shared them with *The New York Times*.

The WikiLeaks versions of the cables initially incorporated redactions. Thereafter, WikiLeaks had to release the cables in unredacted form because the password to decrypt the unredacted files had already been revealed by David Leigh and Luke Harding of *The Guardian* in the book *WikiLeaks: Inside Julian Assange's War on Secrecy* (Leigh124). In an editorial posted to the website on September 1, 2011, WikiLeaks condemned this act of revealing the password as sheer negligence. The incident strained the relationship between WikiLeaks and *The Guardian* (Bellia 1477). The entire turn of events demonstrates that WikiLeaks seeks to maintain a monopoly on information capital with stipulations on what to publish, how much to publish, and when to publish their acquired material. And amidst all this, Assange is the central figure of authority.

Digital networks turn individual users into isolated nodes—every one of them trapped in a bubble of digital preferences. Algorithms direct the flow of targeted advertisements, contact suggestions, and reminders. WikiLeaks intensifies this individualism not by promoting the identities of its individual audience, but by constantly reinforcing Assange identity as a hero facing the wrath of states and corporations. Everything in WikiLeaks is contingent upon him. His portrait appears on the website mastheads. The recent proliferation of Assange's low-angle shots reinforces his messianic identity. He stands at the elevated balcony of the Ecuadorian embassy in London and looks down on the cameras like a hero promising deliverance.

4. CONCLUSION

WikiLeaks marks the rise of an information-based industry, which runs parallel to digital capitalism, and in which information is equivalent to money. WikiLeaks does not directly monetize information, but it uses its control over information to gain political influence according to its September 2011 editorial. It uses the digital labor of whistleblowers, gathers information capital, attains popularity, and sells the popularity for more information capital as well as for commercial profit (seeking donation and selling merchandise, for instance). Although whistleblowers transfer information and do not necessarily produce it, they uncover hidden truths for which Assange eventually takes credit. WikiLeaks makes its contributors agents of surveillance. Absence of advertising and reliance on charitable funding create a non-capitalist image of the organization. This reaffirms Assange's role as the *parrhesiastes* bearing the cross.

Information gathered from whistleblowers also acts as a token of security for the website. The documentary evidence of state atrocities gives WikiLeaks the power to negotiate deals with media institutions and, apparently, to unsettle governments and call them out on their misdeeds (Assange). Individual whistleblowers with identities bound to nation states and corporations are liable to face punitive action for whistleblowing, but WikiLeaks, which functions as an autonomous digital platform without affiliation to any state or organization, cannot be punished for hosting documentary evidence uploaded by others.

Perhaps it is impossible in a networked society for an organization or an individual to form resistance against powerful networks without becoming a powerful network itself. By means of absolute control over its technical resources, WikiLeaks reclaims digital space from governments and corporations but does not entirely transfer the power to individual citizens whom it claims to represent (Assange). It constructs an alternative digital space, a territory of subversion, a borderless utopia of dissent in response to the dystopic surveillance of state and corporations. Nevertheless, it embodies the same principles of control, surveillance, and hegemony. Žižek reflects in his 2014 article in *The Guardian* that WikiLeaks underscores the disturbing absence of freedom in contemporary dystopic society. In my contention, WikiLeaks does it by repressing the freedom of its invisible participants. Although developments in digital technology since Web 2.0 hardly yielded any freedom to individual users, WikiLeaks does not really achieve anything extraordinary in terms of liberating individual users through what Assange identifies in his editorial note dated November 8, 2016 as "public's right to be informed." Instead, it perpetuates dominance over common users by withholding the choice to reveal their identities. Indeed, the organization has given whistleblowers a platform to reveal disturbing secrets about state and corporate affairs, but it maintains its monopolistic hold on the method of dissemination of what it identifies as "public information" (Assange). WikiLeaks representatives have been proactive in securing the protection for Snowden and sending him to Russia in the aftermath of the PRISM leaks (Corbett). However, there is not yet any recognized form of jurisdiction that allows the organization to protect whistleblowers and offer them asylum. Hence, Assange's claim that he protects whistleblowers—vaunted in the WikiLeaks editorial dated November 8, 2016—is misleading. He simply casts the shadow of anonymity on them and basks in reflected glory.

WORKS CITED

Assange, Julian. "Editorial." *WikiLeaks*, 8 Nov. 2016, www.wikileaks.org/Assange-Statement-on-the-US-Election.html. Accessed 27 Dec. 2018.

Bellia, Patricia L. "WikiLeaks and the Institutional Framework for National Security Disclosures." *The Yale Law Journal*, vol. 121, no. 6, Apr. 2012, pp. 1448-1526.

Benjamin, Walter. "Theses on the Philosophy of History." *Illuminations*, edited by Hannah Arendt, translated by Harry Zohn, London, Bodley Head, 1970, pp. 246-255.

Benkler, Yochai. "WikiLeaks and the Networked Fourth Estate." *Beyond WikiLeaks: Implications for the Future of Communications, Journalism and Society*, edited by Benedetta Brevini, Arne Hintz, and Patrick McCurdy, Palgrave Macmillan, 2013.

Corbett, Sara. "How a Snowdenista Kept the NSA Leaker Hidden in a Moscow Airport." *Vogue*, 19 Feb. 2015, www.vogue.com/article/sarah-harrison-edward-snowden-wikileaks-nsa. Accessed 27 Dec. 2018.

Elgot, Jessica. "Edward Snowden: NSA Whistleblower Had to Reveal his Identity or He'd Disappear." *Huffington Post,* 11 Jun. 2013, www.huffingtonpost.co.uk/2013/06/11/edward-snowden-nsa-whistleblower_n_3419750.html. Accessed 18 Oct. 2017.

Foucault, Michel. "Discourse and Truth: The Problematization of Parrhesia." *Six Lectures Given by Michel Foucault at Berkeley*, Oct.-Nov.,1983, pp.1-66, foucault.info/parrhesia/. Accessed 15 Jan. 2018.

Halpern, Sue. "The Nihilism of Julian Assange." *The New York Review of Books*, 13 Jul. 2017, www.nybooks.com/articles/2017/07/13/nihilism-of-julian-assange-WikiLeaks/.Accessed 27 Dec. 2018.

Hunt, Elle. "Julian Assange: Chelsea Manning Clemency Was Bid to Make Life Hard for Me." *The Guardian*, 24 Jan. 2017, www.guardian.com/media/2017/jan/24/julian-assange-WikiLeaks-chelsea-manning-pardon-make-life-hard-the-project.Accessed 10 Mar. 2018.

Greenberg, Andy. "Visa, MasterCard Move to Choke WikiLeaks." *Forbes*, 7 Dec. 2010, www.forbes.com/sites/andygreenberg/2010/12/07/visa-mastercard-move-to-choke-wikileaks/. Accessed 27 Dec. 2018.

Katz, Ian. "Pioneering WikiLeaks Collaboration Ended in Distrust and Legal Threats." *The Guardian*, 5 Feb. 2011, www.theguardian.com

/media/2011/feb/05/WikiLeaks-collaboration-distrust-legal-threats. Accessed 27 Dec. 2018.

Leigh, David, and Luke Harding, editors. "The Cables: Near Lochnagar, Scotland, August 2010." *WikiLeaks: Inside Julian Assange's War on Secrecy*, London: Guardian Books, 2011, pp. 124-131.

Nayar, Pramod K. "WikiLeaks, the New Information Cultures and Digital *Parrhesia*." *Economic and Political Weekly*, 25 Dec. 2010, pp. 27-30.

Ray, Michael. "WikiLeaks." *Encyclopaedia Britannica*, www.britannica.com/topic/WikiLeaks. Accessed 28 Dec. 2018.

Smith, David. "From Liberal Beacon to a Prop for Trump: What Has Happened to WikiLeaks?" *The Guardian*, 14 Oct. 2016, www.theguardian.com/media/2016/oct/14/wiileaks-from-liberal-beacon-to-a-prop-for-trump-what-has-happened. Accessed 10 Oct. 2017.

Thorsen, Einar, Chindu Sreedharan, and Stuart Allan. "WikiLeaks and Whistle-Blowing: The Framing of Bradley Manning." *Beyond WikiLeaks: Implications for the Future of Communications, Journalism and Society*, edited by Benedetta Brevini, Arne Hintz, and Patrick McCurdy, Palgrave Macmillan, 2013.

Topping, Alexandra. "Assange's Embassy Stay in Doubt after Ecuador President's Comments." *The Guardian*, 27 Jul. 2018, www.theguardian.com/media/2018/jul/27/julian-assange-ecuador-embassy-future-london-WikiLeaks. Accessed 28 Dec. 2018.

Valencia, Alexandra. "WikiLeaks' Assange Says Ecuador Seeking to End His Asylum." Reuters. www.reuters.com/article/us-ecuador-assange-asylum/wikileaks-assange-says-ecuador-seeking-to-end-his-asylum-idUSKCN1N32AD. Accessed 28 Dec. 2018.

Žižek, Slavoj. "Good Manners in the Age of WikiLeaks." *London Review of Books*, vol. 33, no. 2, 20 Jan. 2011, www.lrb.co.uk/v33/n02/slavoj-zizek/good-manners-in-the-age-of-WikiLeaks. Accessed 10 Oct. 2018.

Žižek, Slavoj. "How WikiLeaks Opened Our Eyes to the Illusion of Freedom." *The Guardian*, 19 Jun. 2014, www.theguardian.com/commentisfree/2014/jun/19/hypocrisy-freedom-julian-assange-wikileaks. Accessed 12 Jul. 2017.

"WikiLeaks Submissions." *WikiLeaks*, WikiLeaks.org/wiki/WikiLeaks:Submissions. Accessed 28 Dec. 2018.

"About WikiLeaks." *WikiLeaks*, 7 May 2011, WikiLeaks.org/About.html. Accessed 10 Oct. 2018.

"What is WikiLeaks." *WikiLeaks*, 3 Nov. 2015, WikiLeaks.org/What-is-WikiLeaks.html. Accessed 12 Jul. 2017.

"WikiLeaks Editorial: Global *Guardian* Journalist Negligently Disclosed Cablegate Passwords." *WikiLeaks*, September 1, 2011, WikiLeaks.org/Guardian-journalist-negligently.html. Accessed 28 Dec.2018.

The Mold Is the Message: Media Literacy vs. Media Health

YONI VAN DEN EEDE
CENTRE FOR ETHICS AND HUMANISM
FREE UNIVERSITY OF BRUSSELS (VUB)
BRUSSELS, BELGIUM

ABSTRACT: *Expecting that media and/or digital technologies "do" things (Verbeek), we are called upon to take a stance on them, theoretically as well as practically. Media literacy represents one such stance—we are prodded to be literate about media—but there are others. To this extent media literacy is a lens through which we look at issues and that shapes what we see. This becomes particularly clear when we consider another lens, namely, that of media health. While media literacy suggests a rather pragmatic way of doing, making do with what is on offer, the image of media health dramatically alters the starting point: media are seen here as affecting us, even to the extent that we become sick and need to be cured. This image or model of media as somehow related to disease and health is developed in varying degrees of explicitness in the work of Bernard Stiegler and Marshall McLuhan among others. In this paper, we investigate the differences between the media literacy and media health models from a meta vantage point and ask how the lens determines how we view and understand certain problems in relation to media/technologies. We do this by deploying a metaphor ourselves, namely that of mold. Our models are molds. They are understood as a "frame or model around or on which something is formed or shaped," but the connotations of fungal growth helping organic decay and of soil and earth are also at stake. Depending on which meaning we prefer, it might turn out that we do not need to choose between our molds/models: they are interconnected, like mold. On a more theoretical level, we link up the media literacy and media health approaches to two major strands in philosophy of technology, namely to the pragmatist/postphenomenological and transcendentalist/critical streams respectively.*

KEYWORDS: media literacy, media health, postphenomenology, critical theory, pragmatism, disease

Following George Lakoff and Mark Johnson, we have learned that metaphors are central to our lives. Metaphorical structures—which are all about *"understanding and experiencing one kind of thing in terms of another"*—are part and parcel of our thinking process and actions (Lakoff and Johnson 5). That, however, does not foreclose that the *choice* of metaphor can be highly relevant. In fact, because of the centrality of metaphors in our conceptual system, as Lakoff and Johnson go on to demonstrate, that choice is often all the more relevant.

With Peter-Paul Verbeek we have come to expect that media and digital technologies "do" things—a metaphor (Verbeek, *What Things Do*). So, we are called upon to take a stance on them, theoretically as well as practically. Media literacy exemplifies one such stance: we are prodded to be sufficiently literate about media—

another metaphor. Yet there are more, different stances possible. To this extent, media literacy is a lens through which we look at issues. The lens shapes what we see. This becomes particularly clear when we consider another lens, namely that of media health.

TWO LENSES

Although less well represented in the popular consciousness, and usually less formalized under the heading of exactly that term, media health acquired an established reputation as a metaphor for reflecting on technology and media. Both images—media literacy and media health—presuppose a default condition that needs remedy. The ideal types of literacy and health stand for that mirror condition of betterment, of improvement coupled to a kind of normative claim: "we should be literate" or "we should be healthy." Nevertheless, the two perspectives have obviously quite different flavors.

Media literacy is about one's place in the human-made world—a world that is filled with digital media, which are our creations. But because they have become society-wide cultural givens, the individual is faced with the challenge of having to relate to them. One would not have to be literate if it were not for the existence of the written word and its importance in society. It is a matter of dealing with what is there. No one in her right mind would propose to an illiterate, as a solution to her/his problem of not being able to read and write, anything else than to *learn* those skills. Society generally shows no mercy toward people who are unable to read or write. Compare to the provisions—already in themselves sufficiently scarce—made for the physically handicapped. Illiteracy is not a handicap because it can be corrected, preferably through the presence of some educational guidance and certainly, in the first place, given enough personal investment of time and energy. At least, so tends to go the more or less implicit discourse. One simply has to *deal* with the situation of society being organized around written communication. In much the same way, media literacy suggests a rather pragmatic way of doing, "making do" with what is on offer. Media are there, and it is our responsibility to develop an adequate interaction with them.

The image of media health dramatically alters the starting point. It sees media as affecting us to the extent that we become sick and need to be cured. The notions of health and disease, of course, immediately evoke visions of organisms, immune systems, pathogens, toxic substances, medicine, antidotes, vaccines and so on. More fundamentally, the suggestion here is of health being achieved in a battle with that which disrupts it; for example, people who are affected with diseases, from colds to cancer, "fight" their illness. In the case of media health, the health-disrupting elements concern certain uses of media, aspects of media, media constellations, et cetera. Consider the difference with media literacy. Media health is certainly *not* an issue of pragmatically coping with what is on offer—exactly that, namely what is there, is making us sick. Some internal, organic balance may become destabilized by a force coming from the outside. Even in the case of abnormal cell growth, as in tumors, the "external enemy" image still holds, as often cancer is seen to be "caused" by environmental factors or the patient's behavior. Thinking through the metaphor, we could say that the achievement of media health could be pursued along the following paths: evading the pathogen (for example not drinking untreated water), immunizing oneself against it, possibly through inoculation (having once combated a type of flu virus, one is now immune to it) or destroying the pathogen (with antibiotics). In any case, health is attained at the cost of a fragile balancing act.

PRAGMATIST VS. TRANSCENDENTAL

While media literacy incites us to positively—albeit critically—become more media-literate, media health hints more at an idea of, at least partly, being at the mercy of something. Notice the overlap with a fault line that has become apparent in contemporary philosophy of technology: between a pragmatically-pragmatistically oriented strand and a so-called transcendental strand. The pragmatic-pragmatist stream, of which postphenomenology is a prominent representative, formally rejects any transcendentalism, i.e., the endeavor of tracing the essence of technology, looking for "'Technology' with a capital T" (Verbeek 4). Rather, inspired by philosophical pragmatism, postphenomenology wants to study empirically how *t*echnologies with a small "t" come about in practical contexts. Precisely that aspect has raised some suspicion from thinkers situated more within critical and/or even phenomenological traditions, such as Andrew Feenberg in "Peter-Paul Verbeek" and "Making the Gestalt Switch," Pieter Lemmens in "Thinking through Media" and "Love and Realism," Dominic Smith in "Rewriting the Constitution," and Jochem Zwier et al. in "Phenomenology and the Empirical Turn." These authors are concerned that the pragmatist strand has become a bit *too* pragmatic, to the extent that it threatens to relapse straight into instrumentalism. It risks staying oblivious to wider conditioning processes of, indeed, Technology with a capital T—that are not fully empirically mappable and describable and, to that extent, should be designated as transcendental. Media literacy and media health speak for these two streams respectively. Verbeek's calls for positive action—perhaps best epitomized in his title, "Let's Make Things Better," once the slogan of Dutch electronics company Philips—line up with a literacy program: it is in *our* hands. Certain things are not quite yet as they should be, but we can mend them, with the right tools, and if we try our best. The transcendental stream, by contrast, sympathizes with the media health lens that surmises there to be wider, overarching conditions that have an impact upon us, which we do not easily control; in fact, our whole way of looking, experiencing, and living may already be tainted by these conditions… may already be diseased.

SYSTEMIC AND SPECIFIC

Now let me return to the two metaphors. Similar dynamics can be discerned in their evaluation as such. Media literacy is scorned for its purported instrumentality. Although Marshall McLuhan is often seen as a pioneer of media literacy, his son Eric McLuhan can be found to observe, much in the spirit of his father's work, that media are addictive and that "[t]hose engaged in teaching 'media literacy' and other media-training courses are actually in the business of peddling toxic and addictive things to naïve new users/addicts-to-be" (McLuhan, E. 84–85). Indeed, such an observation lines up well with McLuhan's general outlook in which media are an environmental affair—like disease. Media have always already shaped our whole way of perceiving, interpreting and organizing the world, before we deliberately start to think about them—like someone who is ill may no longer have a clear view on her illness, exactly because of the effects of that illness (pain, anguish, despondency). No use of trying to steer another course *within* the diseased framework: that just amounts to staying stuck in the framework. According to Marshall McLuhan, we need nothing less than an anti-environment—offered pre-eminently by art—to counteract the effects of a given media environment. With his images of being afflicted by media and his suggestion that we require something of a counterpoison to restore the balance of the whole system, McLuhan can be cast as a promoter of media health.

A well-known contemporary spokesman for media health is, of course, Bernard Stiegler. His recent work reads like a diagnosis. It expands the more fundamental-philosophical construction work of his earlier *Technics and Time* volumes to an across-the-board cultural critique. Like Derrida, Stiegler speaks of "being-ill" (*States of Shock* 83–84). Or, he refers to "ill-being," specifically "*[a]lgorithmic ill-being*" (*Automatic Society* 25–26, 122), or to "malaise," "spiritual sickness" and "cultural sickness" (*Technics and Time, 3* passim, 109, 155). In Stiegler's view, we are living through a crisis brought on by the proletarianizing effects of market capitalism, in the first instance, but aided by digital technologies. These reduce us to mere consumers, causing us to lose "*savoir-faire*" and "*savoir-vivre*" (*The Re-Enchantment of the World* 35). A majority of people become "disaffected individuals" who are not able to *care* anymore (*Uncontrollable Societies of Disaffected Individuals*). Luckily, technology is a *pharmakon*: poison and cure in one. The same technologies that make us unwell can help to "de-proletarianize" us. This view converges with McLuhan's: although McLuhan calls for *anti-*environments, the latter are still *environments*—it is the same *systemic* force that we require for healing.

Yet, the media health metaphor is not completely problem-free. Media literacy approaches can be criticized from the standpoint of media health, namely that they risk becoming too pragmatic-instrumental. But the reverse is possible as well. Even if media are a *pharmakon*, we can ask: are all media as such *pharmaka* at the same time?[1] Or, are there some types of media, or aspects of media, that are more pathogenic than curative, and vice versa? Is that which makes us sick

---

[1] I am implicitly equating the terms "technology" and "medium" here, largely following McLuhan, who tends to use both interchangeably, but also to a certain extent Stiegler, who analyzes in the framework of his technology analysis types of digital technology that nowadays have become hard to distinguish from what we once more clearly understood as "media" (as for instance in the case of social media).

necessarily exactly the same as that which cures us? The pragmatic-pragmatist strand of philosophy of technology perhaps stays blind to wider ontological conditions, which the transcendental-critical strand then claims to account for, but the wide-angle lens applied by the latter makes us lose sight of specificities. More often than not, one cannot really say "precisely what" and "precisely how" from an ontological perspective.

But even more profoundly, there is the question of defining what disease is—if we care to think through the metaphor even further. Despite some popular and even scientific discourse, health and disease do not just get to *be*. Multiple authors have argued how the mechanical model of disease, still dominant in medicine and science, is faulty to the extent that disease is "mediated" by societal discourses (see for instance Schaffner), social-economic-political factors, psychological conditions, personal life events and so on. In *Why Do People Get Ill?*, Darian Leader and David Corfield relate dramatic stories of people developing illnesses precisely at moments that are significant to them, like the day a loved one died. The physical affliction may be truly there, but the timing and circumstances are a translation or instantiation of *meaning*, of processes and factors that we usually do not consider when discussing, let alone treating, disease. In other words, the condition itself is conditioned. And all of a sudden we are catapulted back into calls for more literacy: if we could just take into account all those manifold, seemingly petty details of how, on a micro scale, people fall ill and conversely convalesce, how they pragmatically cope with what is on offer with what is there, we would probably get a better sense of how health and sickness as such interrelate.

From Health to Literacy and Back: Another Lens

But if health itself, as lens, is a matter of which lens one chooses, then we can expect the same for literacy. The lens of literacy presupposes a whole discursive-societal construction of what we expect literacy to be. Indeed, the other way around, if we stretch media literacy wide enough, deepen it substantially enough, inevitably we must arrive at something resembling media health. It seems to be lenses all the way down. This weird Ouroboros-like dynamic of the two metaphors eventually touching ends— if only we trace them far enough— compels us to ask: are the two metaphors then not more akin than we would have initially suspected? Certainly, almost in a trivial light, and as I already indicated at the start, we must observe that because of their dichotomous build, metaphors spur us on to a *change* of some sort. From media illiteracy we are impelled to move toward media literacy. From media disease it is hoped that we can progress toward media health. So, in a way, both are control paradigms up to a point. While media literacy may be so more openly, and media health cloaks as a more holistic approach, both, by way of their sheer binary core, have a "striving" character.

To an extent, this pre-empts the question: do we have to choose? I think we do not have to, and it may be clear from the above that we actually cannot. Like the pragmatic-pragmatist and transcendental-critical philosophies of technology, the two need each other—although they "themselves" might not have fully realized that yet. Importantly, however, we need to start making the interrelationships clear. A good way of doing this, in my opinion, is by following a kind of reversed Occam's razor: instead of tossing out superfluous models, we could include more in hopes of eventually coming across one that sparks some insight.[2] I want to add a metaphor of my own to the mix, as a sort of transversal line or a third dimension to our two metaphors: *mold*.

Especially the multiplicity of meaning attached to the term is pertinent, I believe. Our models are molds. The Free Dictionary defines mold as a "frame or model around or on which something is formed or shaped."[3] "Model," of course, already has the connotation of "modeled" or "being modelled," but the term "mold" puts it more sharply. Our models mold us into a certain way of thinking, seeing, understanding. This emphasizes the lens aspect of our two metaphors and of any metaphor for that matter. But mold also means fungal growth that helps organic decay. In this sense, mold has a lovely ambiguity to it. No one would say generally that mold in nature is a matter of disease; it is a natural process and that is that. Still, food stuffs that have mold on them, like moldy bread or moldy meat, repel us as a potential danger to our health should we eat them. And yet, we savor blue cheese. Because of the ambiguity, mold in this sense is also a question of careful attention. In opening our fridge and finding an item lightly affected by mold, we need to decide, on the basis of everyday practical wisdom, whether at least parts of the item are still safe to eat—a matter in which, pre-eminently, literacy and health meet.

Digging even deeper, literally, we find yet another meaning: soil, earth. Mold is the ground. Although this brings up a jumble of connotations stretching back into philosophical history that I cannot possibly unravel here, very briefly I can say this, though perhaps somewhat simplistically and naïvely: the ground is where we all go "back" to. In the ground, all distinctions collapse. Finally, here ratios of literacy/illiteracy and health/disease become redundant. The ground "is." In that capacity, it also acts as *back*ground to all our existential strivings—acting as a reminder of not being able to control things at all times and in all circumstances. Media health as well as media literacy may be matters of "letting go" as well. The beautiful phrase attributed to Gustave Flaubert serves to illustrate this: "Le seul moyen de guérir, c'est de se considérer comme guéri." The only way to become cured is to think of yourself as cured. This may be read superficially as a mind trick of sorts situated still within that control paradigm: "think of yourself as cured, and you will be cured!" Of course, it is not that simple. Rather, the phrase attests to something of the reverse—a paradox: in order to heal, one first has to let go of the desire to

---

[2] Kindred pleas for accumulation can be found with Richard Rorty, whose solution for not being able to choose among vocabularies would be to open up toward even more vocabularies, to tell more stories; or Bruno Latour, who in the face of messy, chaotic networks advises to always include more actors.

[3] https://www.thefreedictionary.com/mold

be healed. One cannot simply *want* to be cured and be cured.[4] Health, at this level, "in the ground," demands a form of literacy and vice versa, literacy may or may not be "healthy" in this way. But it is a form of literacy and a form of health that have become aware of, open to, their own metaphorical status. They are things now understood in terms of another and they know this; and those other things, they are so, too, and they know it, too; and so on …

Mold differentiates and equalizes at the same time. This counts for our metaphors. Let us try to be media-literate and/or media-healthy—there is really nothing wrong with that. Let us act and think—be pragmatic and critical. But also, let us act and refuse to act, think and refuse to think. So many lenses, so many options.

Works Cited

Feenberg, Andrew. "Making the Gestalt Switch." *Postphenomenological Investigations: Essays on Human-Technology Relations*, edited by Robert Rosenberger and Peter-Paul Verbeek, Lexington Books, 2015, pp. 229–36.

---. "Peter-Paul Verbeek: Review of 'What Things Do.'" *Human Studies*, vol. 32, no. 2, 2009, pp. 225–28.

Lakoff, George, and Mark Johnson. *Metaphors We Live By*. The University of Chicago Press, 1980.

Leader, Darian, and David Corfield. *Why Do People Get Ill?* Penguin, 2008.

Lemmens, Pieter. "Love and Realism." *Foundations of Science*, vol. 22, no. 2, 2017, pp. 305–10.

---. "Thinking Through Media: Stieglerian Remarks on a Possible Postphenomenology of Media." *Postphenomenology and Media: Essays on Human–Media–World Relations*, edited by Yoni Van Den Eede et al., Lexington Books, 2017, pp. 185–206.

McLuhan, Eric. "Concerning Media Ecology." *Valuation and Media Ecology: Ethics, Morals, and Laws*, edited by Corey Anton, Hampton Press, 2010, pp. 75–88.

McLuhan, Marshall. "The Relation of Environment to Anti-Environment." *The Human Dialogue: Perspectives on Communication*, edited by Floyd W. Matson and Ashley Montagu, Free Press, 1967, pp. 39–47.

Schaffner, Anna Katharina. *Exhaustion: A History*. Columbia University Press, 2016.

Smith, Dominic. "Rewriting the Constitution: A Critique of 'Postphenomenology.'" *Philosophy & Technology*, vol. 28, no. 4, 2015, pp. 533–51.

Stiegler, Bernard. *Automatic Society, Volume 1: The Future of Work*. Translated by Daniel Ross, Polity, 2016.

---

[4] Stiegler begins to convey this sentiment, notwithstanding his overall lens of "sickness" and "cure" and the tension between them when he refers, for instance, with Deleuze, to "the whole *positive play of illness and health*" (quoted in Stiegler, *States of Shock* 67; original emphasis) and, with Canguilhem, to "*the power and the will to fall sick*" (quoted in Stiegler, *States of Shock* 61; original emphasis). Of course, the notion of *pharmakon*, poison and cure in one, as such implies a tight interrelation between disease and health. Then again, there is the general thrust in Stiegler's work to *go from*, to *move from* ill-being *to* well-being.

---. *States of Shock: Stupidity and Knowledge in the 21st Century*. Translated by Daniel Ross, Polity, 2015.

---. *Technics and Time, 3: Cinematic Time and the Question of Malaise*. Translated by Stephen Barker, Stanford University Press, 2011.

---. *The Re-Enchantment of the World: The Value of Spirit Against Industrial Populism*. Translated by Trevor Arthur, Bloomsbury, 2014.

---. *Uncontrollable Societies of Disaffected Individuals: Disbelief and Discredit, Volume 2*. Translated by Daniel Ross, Polity, 2013.

Verbeek, Peter-Paul. "Let's Make Things Better: A Reply to My Readers." *Human Studies*, vol. 32, no. 2, 2009, pp. 251–61.

---. *What Things Do: Philosophical Reflections on Technology, Agency, and Design*. Translated by Robert P. Crease, The Pennsylvania State University Press, 2005.

Zwier, Jochem, et al. "Phenomenology and the Empirical Turn: A Phenomenological Analysis of Postphenomenology." *Philosophy & Technology*, vol. 29, no. 4, 2016, pp. 313–33.

Contributors

ALBERTO JOSÉ LUIS CARRILLO CANÁN received his doctorate in philosophy from the Free University in Berlin, Germany. He is a full professor and researcher at the Benemérita Universidad Autónoma de Puebla and is responsible for a corpus of academic work on aesthetics and media. His research encompasses aesthetics, media theory, philosophy of technology, cognitive sciences, and history of science.

JOÃO CARLOS CORREIA holds Habilitation and Ph.D. from University of Beira Interior where he is an Associate Professor in Communication Sciences. Professor Correia has been the Chair of I & D Unit Research Communication until 2017 and is now the Editor of *Communication Studies* (indexed in Scopus), a lead researcher at Regional Media Lab & Incubator (2018-2021), Philosophy and Humanities, and the Chair of Political Communication WG from Portuguese Society of Communication since 2017. His main interests are in the politics of communication, net activism, and critical theory. Among his recent works were the following book chapters: "Structural Crises of Meaning and New Technologies: Reframing the Public and the Private News Media through the Expansion of Voices by Social Networks" coauthored with Ana Serrano Tellería and Heitor Costa Lima da Rocha (Rutledge 2017); "Mass, Publics and Multitudes: Digital Activism and Its Paradoxes" (Peter Lang 2015); "Le rôle des réseaux socionumériques dans la configuration épistémologique des societé" (Press Universitaires du Québeq 2014).

ULAŞ BAŞAR GEZGIN is a journalist, a social science researcher, and an academic who holds degrees in education, psychology, cognitive science, and urban planning. He has research experience in New Zealand, Australia, and Latin America and has taught various institutions in Turkey, Vietnam, Thailand, and Malaysia. Dr Gezgin has published widely in and outside of academia: in addition to numerable book chapters and journal articles in various fields, he has published a novel, an opera libretto, edited collections of poetry, a compilation of short stories, textbooks and translations. His work has been translated to 11 languages: English, French, German, Spanish, Italian, Russian, Japanese, Vietnamese, Thai, Georgian, and Azerbaijani.

STACEY O'NEIL IRWIN is a Media and Broadcasting Professor at Millersville University of Pennsylvania. Her first book *Digital Media: Human-Media Relations* (2016) was published by Lexington Books. A follow-up text, *Postphenomenology and Media: Essays on Human–Media–World Relations* (2017) edited with Yoni Van Den Eede and Galit Wellner was also published by Lexington Books.

OLGA KUDINA holds a Ph.D. in philosophy of technology from the University of Twente, the Netherlands. Her dissertation explores the way technologies co-shape human values, highlighting the technologically mediated formation of meaning in this regard. Her research interests include ethics of emerging technologies, (post)phenomenology, hermeneutics, and bioethics. This work was supported by the Netherlands Organization for Scientific Research (NWO) under a research program "Theorizing Technological Mediation: Toward an Empirical-Philosophical Theory of Technology," project number 277-20-006.

PAUL MAJKUT is a Professor of Literature and Philosophy at National University. He writes on media change and is actively involved in the struggle against racism, fascism, and anarcho-libertarianism. Professor Majkut is the founder of SPM.

NYASHA MBOTI is an Associate Professor in the Department of Communication Studies at the University of Johannesburg. Professor Mboti is currently researching possibilities for the emergence of Apartheid Studies as a new theoretical paradigm. He has been invited to deliver the keynote address at the 2018 SPM Conference in Akureyri, Iceland.

RIANKA ROY is an Assistant Professor of English at Surendranath College for Women at the University of Calcutta. She has submitted her doctoral thesis on social media surveillance at School of Media, Communication and Culture at Jadavpur University. She continues her research on digital labor, digital privacy, social media security and digital workplace.

YONI VAN DEN EEDE's research concerns philosophy of technology and media ecology with an emphasis on phenomenological, cultural, existential, and political themes. He is among others the author of *Amor Technologiae* (VUB Press 2012) and the co-editor of *Postphenomenology and Media* (Lexington Books 2017). He is a Director of SPM since 2011 and, served as SPM President from 2014 to 2016.

www.ingramcontent.com/pod-product-compliance
Lightning Source LLC
Chambersburg PA
CBHW081013040426
42444CB00014B/3197